...New York.

Get the Agent you need for the career you want

K CALLAN

Seventh Edition 2004
First Printing
Other Editions 1987, 1990, 1993, 1995, 1998, 2001
ISBN 1-878355-16-3
ISSN 1058-1928

Illustrations: Katie Maratta
Map: Kelly Callan
Photography: Don Williams
Editor: Daniel Curran

K Callan Can Make Your Career

I hope that got your attention. Because *this very second* you have the chance to do one thing that will instantly increase your chances of "making it."

Buy. This. Book.

Within the pages of the seventh (the Seventh!) edition of *The New York Agent Book*, you will find everything you need to succeed in the Biz's first and most intimidating hurdle: How to get an agent.

Who are the

agent with one of New York's finest agencies, DGRW, home to the legendary and sorely missed Barry Douglas and Fred Gorman; the queen of contract, Flo Rothacker; and my mentor, Jim Wilhelm. The brilliant and dedicated Michelle Gerard and Josh Pultz joined later.

Like many beginning agents, I was making the rounds of the various seminar companies in NYC. If you're reading this book you probably already know the drill. Pay your money and get to audition for a real live (fill in the blank) agent, casting director, or manager.

I was astonished by how little these beginning actors knew about the business. As talented as some of them were, they were as far from being able to take the necessary professional steps to success as I was from being able to sing "Bring Him Home."

I did what little I could to pass on what I knew, but one day at our daily meeting, I mentioned how frustrated I was about how little people seemed to know. "Isn't there some book they could read?"

And that's when I met K the author. I think it was Flo (who is quoted in this book – words to live by) who reminded me of *The New York Agent Book*. She had a copy (I say "had" because I promptly stole it, sorry Flo) which became my Bible.

And what a Bible it is. All the questions you might have, and just as importantly, all the questions *you should have* are brought up and discussed.

How should you dress for a meeting?

Covered.

What do agents look for (the twenty dollar question)?

Covered.

When is it time to look for a new agent? (The ten dollar question – since ten will go to the old agent. Sorry. Agent humor).

Covered. Covered. Covered.

Unlike most authors of books for actors, K speaks from experience as a successful working actress in an increasingly difficult and complex business. You've seen her in *Lois and Clark* (as the real Ma Kent), *JAG, Coach,* and most recently as the heart-rending Okie in HBO's *Carnivale.* She's lived the actor's life, to the utmost. And when she chose to share what she had learned, she made it that much easier for the rest of you.

Don't take my word for it. Try this simple test. Close the book. Open it randomly three times. I guarantee you'll learn three things not only that you didn't know before, but that *you need to know.* Try it. I'll wait.

Done? Okay. One more thing.

Buy. This. Book.

K Callan can make your career.

It's as simple as that.

Andy Lawler, ex-agent DGRW
General Manager of Charlotte Repertory Company

⚖ Introduction ⚖

Directors, producers, agents and civilians (people not in the business) frequently comment to me that my books about the entertainment industry follow a circuitous route. Actors never say that. They know the business *is* a circuitous route. You enter the circle anyplace and usually don't get to choose where. It is possible to spend twenty years at this occupation and still feel like a beginner, depending on what phase of the career you are experiencing.

Th̶ ̶̶̶̶̶̶ ̶ ̶̶̶̶ ̶

̶̶̶̶̶̶ ̶̶̶̶̶ ̶̶̶ ̶̶̶ ̶̶̶ ̶̶̶̶ ̶̶̶ ̶̶̶̶̶̶ ̶̶̶̶ ̶̶̶ ̶̶̶ ̶̶̶̶̶̶̶ ̶̶ ̶̶ ̶̶ ̶̶̶̶̶̶̶ ̶̶ ̶̶ turns out. We all just take them at different times.

As important as business skills is self-knowledge. Although some actors never have to find a niche for themselves, most of us spend several years figuring out just what it is we have to sell. If you weigh 500 pounds, it doesn't take a master's degree to figure out that you're going to play the fat one. If you go on a diet and become a more average size, casting directors will have a harder time pegging which one you are and you may, too. This is not to say that if you are easily typed that your life is a bed of roses, but it can be a lot easier.

So, *Self-Knowledge* could be the first chapter for one actor and the end of the book for another. An actor who already has an agent might feel justified in starting with chapter eleven because he wants to change agents while a newcomer in town might feel that divorce is not the problem he's currently confronted with. At this point, all he wants is an agent — any agent.

In fact, a beginning actor would gain insight from chapter eleven. That information could alert him to potential warning signs when he *is* meeting with an agent and chapter two might prompt the seasoned actor to reexamine all the things his agent does do for him.

This book deals with all aspects of actor/agent relationships at various stages of one's career: the first agent, the freelance alliance, the exclusive relationship, confronting the agent with problems, salvaging the bond, and if need be, leaving the partnership.

There is information for the newcomer, help for the seasoned actor and encouragement for everybody. Interviewing hundreds of agents in New York and Los Angeles was just like every other part of the business, sometimes scary, sometimes wonderful and sometimes painful, but always a challenge.

Mostly, the agents were funny, interesting, dynamic, warm and not at all as unapproachable as they seem when you are outside the office looking in.

Regardless of the circuitous nature of the business and this book, my strong advice to you is to read *straight through* and not skip around. The first part provides background to critically understanding the information in the latter part of the book.

Fight the urge to run to the agency listings and read about this agent or that. Until you digest more criteria regarding evaluating agents you may find yourself just as confused as before.

If you read the agents' words with some perception, you will gain insights not only into their character but into how the business really runs. You will notice whose philosophy coincides with yours. Taken by themselves the quotations might only be interesting, but considered in context and played against the insights of other agents, they are revealing and educational.

I have quoted a few agents that you will not find listed here because they are either from Los Angeles (Ken Kaplan, Tim Angle), out of the business (Joanna Ross, Lynn Moore Oliver) or deceased (Michael Kingman, Barry Douglas). Even though you won't be able to consider them as possible business partners, I felt their insights were particularly valuable.

Check all addresses before mailing. Every effort has been made to provide accurate and current addresses and phone numbers, but agents move and computers goof. Call the office and verify the address, and make sure the agent you want to contact is still there.

It's been a gratifying experience to come in contact with all the agents and all the actors I have met as a result of my books. Because I am asking the questions for all of us, if I've missed something you deem important, tell me and I'll include it in my next book. Write to me c/o Sweden Press at the address on the back of the book, or at my e-mail address: Kcallan@swedenpress.com. Be sure to write something in the reference line that identifies you as a reader; I dump a lot of junk mail.

K Callan
Los Angeles, California

⚓ Table of Contents ⚓

⚔ 1 ⚔
Forewarned

The 6th Edition of this book rolled off the presses in 2001 and, in the meantime, the world and the business continues to change.

~~Union issues cast a veil of uncertainty over the future of the Screen~~

~~As SAG president,~~ in October 2003, she announced that the SAG/AFTRA merger is the first item on her agenda. There will be resistance, but this may be an idea whose time has finally come.

And the business, as all other things, continues to change.

✦ *I think the business has changed, but not just because of 9/11 and the strike. It was changing before that. Today stars get everything, all the big roles, all the small roles, all the cameos. I keep hoping "stunt castings" a phase but I'm afraid it isn't. As companies merge and wield broader power, the "safe" choice is treasured all the more.*
Dianne Busch/Leading Artists, Inc.

I agree with Diane, the business is merely reflecting the nation as a whole. We live in a corporate world leaving little room for all but big business.

Consider all the mom & pop bookstores replaced by Barnes & Noble, the neighborhood hardware stores erased by Home Depot. Log onto www.abc.com, www.nbc.com, www.cbs.com, etc., and check out the program schedule. The number of reality shows in one form or another is staggering. *Trading Spaces, Queer Eye for the Straight Guy,* and *Extreme Make-over* are just the tip of the iceberg.

Cheap to produce, topical, and growing in popularity, every time you see a time slot filled with a reality show, that's an actor-free time slot.

As with any business, the way to survive and prosper is to see how you can use the energy of the marketplace to your advantage. If you were a saddle maker when automobiles were invented, you could whine and ask for a subsidy or you could figure out how to adapt your business to the new world.

That's what actors have to do now. Perhaps you'll be lucky and find a place in the marketplace without adapting, but maybe there is a way for you to create a show that will fit into the current climate.

Oprah studied to be an actress, switched to media and began a career as a broadcaster which led her to an Academy Award nomination for *The Color Purple* among countless other showbiz accomplishments. You never know where your entrepreneurial talents will take you. The one thing we know is true is that an investment of positive energy always pays off.

Forearmed

With that in mind, whether you're just starting in the business and are just trying to figure out your first step, or whether you find yourself agent-less, take heart and take a big breath. Anything is possible.

Let's begin.

Change

✓ continues
✓ sink or swim, it's up to you

↘ 2 ↙
Avenues of Opportunity

Many actors regularly curse and malign agents. They either feel rejected that they can't get an agent to talk to them or frustrated once they have an agent simply because of their unrealistic expectations.

to sign me, how can I choose the right one? If no one wants to sign me, what will I tell my mother?

Let's dispense with the mother issue right off. Unless your mother is an actress, she is never going to understand. Those who have never pursued a job in show business (civilians and would-be actors who are still in school) can never understand what an actor goes through in pursuit of employment and/or an agent. So don't waste time on that conversation.

Just say: "Mom, I'm doing great. I'm unemployed right now and I don't have an agent, but that's part of the process. There are things I need to accomplish before it's time for me to look for an agent."

She can repeat that to her friends. She's still not going to understand, but it will mean something to her that you have a plan.

What Is An Agent?

Whether your agent fantasy includes the old-fashioned stereotype of cigar-chomping hustlers or the newer version of the cool customer in the expensive suit, many actors fantasize that the right agent holds the secret of success. Ex-WMA agent, Joanna Ross, left the business and moved to Italy, but I'm still quoting her because her perspective on the actor/agent relationship is so insightful.

◆ *Actors feel that if they make the right choice, the agent is somehow going to make them a star and help them be successful, or they're going to make the wrong choice and that's it. And that's just not it.*

No agent can make anybody a star or make him a better actor than he is. Agents are only avenues of opportunity.
Joanna Ross

That being the case, what do these "Avenues of Opportunity" do? The dictionary (which knows very little about show business) has several definitions for the word "agent." By combining a couple, I've come up with one that works for show business: A force acting in place of another, effecting a certain result by driving, inciting, or setting in motion.

Huh?

In its simplest incarnation, the agent, acting on your behalf, sets in motion a series of events that result in your having a shot at a job. He gets you meetings, interviews, and auditions. And he prays that you will get the job or at the very least make him look good by being brilliant at your audition.

When an actor grouses that the agent is not getting him out, he seems to think the agent doesn't want him to work, completely forgetting that if the actor doesn't work, the agent cannot pay his rent. Not only that, the actor overlooks the fact that his part of the partnership is to get the job.

It should be simple to get the job, really. After all, you have spent years studying; perfecting your instrument; training your body, voice, craft, defining your personality; and building a resume that denotes credibility. Haven't you?

An Agent Prepares

While you have been working on every aspect of your craft, an agent has spent his time getting to know the business. He's seen every play, television show, and film. He's watched actors, writers, directors, and producers birth their careers and grow. He's tracked people at every level of the business. He has networked, stayed visible, and communicated. He's made it his business to meet and develop relationships with casting directors, or CDs, as they are sometimes referred to throughout this book.

The agent you want only represents those actors whose work he personally knows so that when he tells a casting director that an actor is perfect for the role and has the background for it, the casting director trusts his word. That's the way the agent builds credibility. It doesn't happen any faster than the building of the actor's resume.

In addition to getting the actor the appropriate audition, the agent has to be prepared to negotiate a brilliant contract when the actor wins the job. That entails knowing all the rules and regulations of the Screen Actors Guild, Actors' Equity, and American Federation of Television and Radio Artists, as well as having an understanding of the

What Do Agents Think Their Job Is?

✦ *I feel that I'm responsible for my clients' attitudes and for their self-confidence.*
Kenneth Kaplan/The Gersh Agency, Inc.

✦ *If you sign someone, if you agree to be their agent, no matter how big the agency gets, you've agreed to be there for them and that's your responsibility.*
Kenneth Kaplan/The Gersh Agency, Inc.

✦ *If someone puts their trust in me, then I need to help them earn a living. I want to get them work. I want actors who are talented, but I have to like them.*
Marvin Josephson/Gilla Roos, Ltd.

✦ *Sometimes actors don't really consider all the work an agent may do for them that doesn't result in an appointment. The agent may have said your name many times to the casting director until the CD has heard it often enough that he begins to think you are actually working.*

At that point, the actor happens to call the casting director himself and ends up with an appointment and subsequently a job. Now he calls his agent and says, "Well, hey. I got the job myself. Why should I pay you commission?"

In my head, I'm going, "Who sat down with you and told you how to dress? Who helped you select the photos you are using right now that got you that audition? Who helped you texture your resume? Who introduced you to the casting director?

What makes you think you did that on your own?"

They don't see it. They don't see that, like a manager, I have taken them from here to there. I set up the auditions. Most actors don't realize the initial investment we make, the time, the energy, the phone calls, the mail, the hours of preparing the actor and getting them to the right places. There is no compensation for that until maybe two years down the road.

At that point, you've made them so good that someone else signs them anyway. There's not a lot of loyalty among actors. They'll always want the person who gets them the next job. They don't comprehend what we go through to get them ready for that point where they can get a job.
H. Shep Pamplin/Agents for the Arts, Inc.

Try to digest the truth of Shep's statement. It is an unusual person who arrives on the scene poised enough to handle himself in the audition room. That kind of poise usually cannot be acquired without going through the struggle time. An agent who invests his time and energy in the struggle time should be rewarded, not discarded.

✦ *I offer hard work and honesty and demand the same in return. If I'm breaking my ass to get you an audition, you better show up.*
Martin Gage/The Gage Group

Although it might be nice to be pals with your agent, it is not necessary. One of the best agents I ever had was never available to help me feel good when all was dark. He did, however, initiate new business for me, was respected in the community, negotiated well, showed impeccable taste, and had access to everyone in the business.

He also believed in me and retained that faith when I did not win every audition. He gave me good notes on my performances, clued me in to mistakes I was making, and made a point of viewing my work at every opportunity.

Oh yes, and he returned my phone calls!

A friend of mine, who toiled for many years on a well-regarded series, was happy to be working, but felt her agent had not negotiated well. She changed agents and doubled her salary. A year later, she changed agents again: "They were good negotiators, but I couldn't stand talking to them."

You can't have everything.

Being a tough negotiator sometimes displaces graciousness. So maybe your agent won't be your best friend. He's not supposed to be, he's your business partner. You have to decide what you want and what you need.

Ex-Los Angeles agent, Lynn Moore Oliver, offers a comprehensive picture of what agents are doing on our behalf, even when we can't tell they are even thinking about us.

✦ *I'm working on the belief that symbiotically we're going to build a career. While the actor isn't working, I'm paying for the phone, the stationery, the envelopes, the Breakdown Service (which is expensive), the messenger service to send the pictures*

and I've probably invested more money in the actor's career than he has, on an annual basis.
Lynn Moore Oliver

If you think about what Lynn says, you will understand why credible agents choose clients carefully. Looking at your actor friends, are there any that you would be willing to put on your list and pay to promote? Puts things more in perspective, doesn't it?

Franchised Agents or Not?

The terms of agreement between the ATA and SAG are currently in a state of flux since 2002 when SAG members voted down an ATA proposed new agreement. Since the terms of the original agreement have been the same for forty years, it really is time to reflect the evolving marketplace and give assistance to smaller, mid-level agencies.

Although conglomerates like William Morris, ICM, CAA, etc. that represent actors with million dollar paychecks have no problem paying their rent, the existence of agencies representing working actors is threatened.

Management's refusal to pay working actors much over scale, plus competition from managers who have the ability to produce and can charge a higher commission, has put many smaller agencies out of business. So it's possible that some restrictions will ease and that agents will soon be charging more than 10%.

These changes are long overdue and agents deserve our support in this fight. Stay focused on business. Educate yourself so that you can make intelligent decisions in the partnership between you and your agent.

♦ *Independent talent agencies (i.e., those agencies that are not affiliated with either the Association of Talent Agents [ATA] and/or the National Association of Talent Representatives [NATR]) continue to be franchised and regulated by the SAG Franchise Agreement [or, Rule 16(g)], the Agreement that has regulated your relationship with your SAG agent for the last 63 years. Accordingly, so long as your agency abides by the terms and conditions of Rule 16(g), it may continue to represent you. Any standard SAG agency contract you sign with an independent agency may be filed with, and processed by, the Guild. If your independent agency chooses to surrender its franchise with the Guild, SAG will immediately notify you of that fact.*

SAG's franchises with agents that are members of the ATA and/or NATR have ended. However, pending further review, SAG's National Board of Directors has temporarily suspended application of Rule 16(a) of the Rules and Regulations section of the SAG Constitution, which requires SAG members to be represented only by a franchised agent. Because of this temporary suspension, a SAG member may continue to be represented by one of these formerly franchised agents.

For those members who are contemplating signing new contracts with their ATA/NATR agents, you should insist, whenever possible, upon the standard SAG representation contract or a contract whose terms and conditions mirror those in (or are better than) Rule 16(g).

www.sag.org

If your agent hands you a General Services Agreement to sign, do take SAG up on their offer to go over it with you and offer advice. Most agents will not require that you agree with every single line in the contract.

At this point, the only thing the agent must do is have a license to operate from the state. The license addresses about 10% of the areas covered by the agreement hammered out by SAG. So just because an agent says, "Hey, we're fine, we're licensed by the state," doesn't constitute much protection for the actor. Neither this nor the old franchise agreement guaranteed the agent to be ethical, knowledgeable or effective. You'll have to check that yourself.

Wrap Up

Agent

✓ a force acting in place of another, effecting a certain result by driving, inciting, or setting in motion

✓ no longer formally regulated by SAG

3
First Steps

There's good news and bad news. First the bad news: you're probably going to have to be your own first agent. Now the good news: nobody cares more about your career than you do, so your first agent is going to be incredibly motivated.

In order to attract an agent, you have to have something to sell. No matter how talented you are, if you don't have some way to show what you've got, you're all talk. Working up a scene for the agent's office will work for a few agents, but basically, it's not enough.

Your focus at this point is to amass credits by appearing onstage so an agent can see you, or working in student and independent films, so you can put together a professional audition tape and refine your acting skills. *The New York Agent Book* is focused on actors who are already entrepreneurial. For those who need help in that department, get my marketing book, *How to Sell Yourself as an Actor*.

I know what you are thinking: "Swell. How am I going to amass credits and put together a professional tape without an agent? How am I ever going to get any work? How will I get smarter?"

By taking action. By acting 'as if.' Pick up *Back Stage* or *Show Business* for casting notices. Get on to the actor's grapevine by joining a theater group or getting into an acting class.

◆ *Grab a "Back Stage" and start auditioning for everything! Then, find a well-known and respected acting teacher who works with accomplished students. These two small actions will be the beginning of your show business networking. Teachers, friends and colleagues provide a conduit to your future agent or to a casting director.*
Jeanne Nicolosi/Nicolosi & Co., Inc.

◆ *Contact everyone you know. Get to class. Get good headshots. If you are "soap" material, send your picture/resume to all the daytime casting directors.*
Diana Doussant/HWA

◆ *I would go to class. I would do anything I could. I would not sit around feeling sorry for myself. If I couldn't get someone to hire me as an actor, I'd get a group of my friends in the same position, move all the furniture to one side and do a play in*

my living room and then call the agents and ask them to come see me.
Lionel Larner/Lionel Larner, Ltd.

That's exactly what Carol Burnett did when she first came to New York. Read her bio, *One More Time*, for inspiration.

Preparation

In order to agent yourself, you will need to do all the things we

selling programs, or candy, or watching the phone or the stage door. I would get myself a job in the business because you learn a tremendous amount. I also think it shows the determination because you're not looking immediately for the reward before doing the work. We all have to pay our dues.
Lionel Larner/Lionel Larner, Ltd.

The Actor's Job: Looking for Work

Becoming an actor is not an overnight process. A large part of being an actor on any level is looking for work. Don't equate being paid with being an actor.

You are already an actor. Even if you are a student actor, you're still an actor and you actually have your first assignment: get a resume with decent credits. This will not only begin to season you as an actor, but if it's on film, you will be able to start building an audition tape.

What denotes decent credits? Although agents are happy to see school and hometown credits on a resume so they know you've actually had some time onstage, those credits not only don't mean much in the marketplaces of LA/NYC/Chicago, they don't constitute an arena for the agent to see you in action, first hand.

If, on the other hand, you are appearing in a decent venue where an agent can drop by and look at you or, if he is canvassing the town on his own, discover you, then you have the possibility of becoming a marketable commodity.

When you can also deliver an example of your work on videotape (an audition tape), you are in business. The tape is usually no longer than five minutes and shows either one performance or a montage of scenes of an actor's work.

Agents and casting executives view tapes endlessly and can tell quickly if you are of interest to them, so even if you have some great stuff, err on the side of brevity. It is better to have just one good scene from an actual job than many short moments of work or a scene produced just for the reel. Some agents will watch self-produced work on a reel and some will not. Some casting directors tell me they usually watch whatever is sent.

Agents and casting directors prefer to see tapes featuring professional appearances on television or film, though some will look at a tape produced solely for audition purposes.

If you can't produce footage that shows you clearly in contemporary material playing a part that you could logically be cast for, then you aren't far enough along to make a tape. Better to wait than to show yourself at less than your best. Patience.

What Casting Directors and Agents Want in a Picture

The number one dictate from casting directors about pictures is: What You See Is What You Get. Casting directors don't like surprises. If your picture looks like Jennifer Lopez and you look like Joan Cusack, the casting director is not going to be happy when he calls you in to read. And vice versa.

Your picture and your reel are your main selling tools, so choose carefully. Pictures can be printed with or without a border. Some agents prefer a picture without, but borderless frequently costs more. Your name can printed on the front or not, either superimposed over the photo or in the white space below. Casting directors just care that the picture looks like you.

Pictures

There are many good photographers in town who make a business of taking actors' headshots. They vary in price and product. I've gathered a list of favorites from agents, actors, and casting directors.

Don't just choose one off the list. You need to do your own research on something as personal as a photograph.

Make an appointment with at least three photographers to evaluate their book and how comfortable you feel with them. No matter how good the pictures, if you don't feel at ease with that person, your pictures are going to reflect that. Take the time to evaluate your compatibility.

The Internet has made shopping for a photographer easier. Not only do many photographers have their own web pages (type in the

pay $400-$450 for pictures. Some photographers include hair and make-up artists as part of their package. That's nice, but make sure you can duplicate the look when you audition.

It's not just a question of hair and make-up, it's about the photographer understanding your essence. A friend of mine had some pictures taken by a respected Los Angeles photographer. The pictures were technically perfect, but there was a darkness to them that had nothing to do with the natural affability of my friend. The shadowy mood pictures are interesting, but have nothing to do with who he is and how he will be cast.

Photographers & What They Charge

My list of photographers was gleaned by quizzing agents and actors for recommendations. From that list, I called a few to get an idea of prices.

Richard Blinkoff, for instance, has a special price for clients age sixteen and under. Since he feels that kids need pictures more often than you and me, he charges them $250 for two rolls of 36 pictures each and they receive one custom 8x10 for copying. Adults pay $350 for the same package but get an additional 8x10. Call him at 212-620-7883 or view his work at www.tvistudios.com/gallery/showPhot.asp?photID=2.

Tess Steinkolk sounds just great. She graduated from the American

University in Washington D.C., a city in which she had an illustrious career not only at the White House during the Carter Administration but at the Smithsonian where she studied and was also on staff. During that time she was also house photographer for the Arena Stage. She moved to New York in 1981 and continues her amazing work.

Tess charges $545 for a three-roll session and gives you two 8x10s and will sell her original negs for $125 each. Her prices escalate to $675 for five rolls and four 8x10s. She has a special teen/kids price of $425 for two rolls with two 8x10s. There is a $75 discount for cash payment.

Her web page features her pictures and other important information so check her out at www.tsteinkolk.com/home.html or call 212-627-1366.

Dave Cross has been a professional photographer in New York for the last twelve years. After five years as an actor he decided to photograph actors instead of being one. In addition to shooting Broadway, soaps, movie performers and theater companies, Cross' work has been seen in the *New York Times, Time-Out Magazine, Dance Magazine* and *Soap Opera Digest*.

He shoots digitally and charges $625 for 150-200 images. You see the shots during the session and have a contact sheet the next day. You get two final images on a CD ready to be duplicated. There's a $25 charge for extra images, $50 to upload the session to your computer. View his work at www.davecrossphotography.com or call him at 212-270-6691.

Barbara Bordnick began her career in Paris and Copenhagen. During a career of more than twenty-five years, she has garnered awards for outstanding work in film, print, advertising and art. Her images are in the permanent collections of the International Center of Photography, the Gilman Collection in New York and the Polaroid Collection in Massachusetts.

She's really a fashion and portrait celebrity photographer so she is pricey at $850 for headshots which includes two wardrobe changes and two prints. Give her a call at 212-505-7879. Check out her work at www.pdnonline.com/masters/MasterBarbara.

Another highly touted photographer is Bill Morris. His headshot package is $325 for a two look shoot. Additional looks are $95 each. Each look includes a retouched master print. His makeup artist charges $150.

Bill shoots high quality digital photography, so you see before he actually starts and you get proofs instantly. Call him at 212-274-1177 and check out his work at www.billmorris.com/html/Pages/info.html.

Jinsey Dauk started shooting pictures in the 8th grade. She studied and then taught photography at Wake Forest University in Winston-Salem, North Carolina and also studied film production and psychiatry. Dauk is also a working actress and model.

Her web page is worth a look at www.jinsey.com. There's a $300 discount for checking out her work there instead of in her apartment/studio so instead of paying $795 for at least three rolls and one 8x10, it's $495. Her phone number is 212-243-0652.

Van Williams says he's too old to have a web page or a cell phone but I can tell you that his pictures are still great. A picture he took in

A resume is sent along with your 8x10 glossy or matte print. Your resume should be stapled to the back so that as you turn the picture over side to side, you see the resume as though it were printed on the back of the photo. The buyers see hundreds of resumes every day, so make yours simple and easy to read.

It's not necessary to have millions of jobs listed. When prospective employers see too much writing, their eyes glaze over and they won't read anything, so be brief.

Choose the most impressive credits and list them. There is an example on the next page to use as a guide. Lead with your strong suit. If you have done more commercials than anything else, list that as your first category; if you are a singer, list music. You may live in a market where theater credits are taken very seriously. If this is so, even though you may have done more commercials, lead with theater if you have anything credible to report.

Adapt this example to meet your needs. If all you have done is college theater, list that. This is more than someone else has done and it will give the buyer an idea of parts you can play. Note that you were master of ceremonies for your town's Pioneer Day Celebration. If you sang at The Lion's Club program, list that. Accomplishments that

John Smith/212-555-4489

6'2" 200 lbs, blonde hair, blue eyes

Theater

Take Me Out .... directed by Joe Mantello
Lost in Yonkers .... directed by Gene Saks

Film

Chuck & Buck .... directed by Miguel Arteta
The Tao of Steve .... directed by Jenniphr Goodwin
How to Lose a Guy in 10 Days .... directed by Donald Petrie

Television

Ed .... directed by Justin Chinn
Law and Order .... directed by Gwen Arner
Third Watch .... directed by Christopher Chulack

Training

Acting .... Karen Ludwig, William Esper, Sam Schacht
Singing .... Andrea Green, Maryann Chalis
Dance .... Andy Blankenbuehler, Christopher Gattelli

Special Skills

guitar, horseback riding, martial arts, street performer, Irish, Spanish, British, Cockney, & French dialect, broadsword, fencing, certified Yoga instructor, circus skills, etc.

might seem trivial to you could be important to someone else, particularly if you phrase it right. If you are truly beginning and have nothing on your resume, at least list your training and a physical description along with the names of your teachers. Younger actors aren't expected to have credits.

The most important thing on your resume is your name and your agent's phone number. If you don't have an agent, get voice mail for work calls. Don't use your personal phone number, it's more professional and it's safer.

so that agents/CDs will have clues on how to cast you.

If you were in a production of *A Streetcar Named Desire* and you played Blanche, by all means say so. If you were a neighbor, say that. The CD or agent wants to know how much work you have actually done; if you have "carried" a show, that's important.

Misrepresenting your work on a resume is self-destructive. You not only risk running into the casting director for that show who will tell you that she doesn't recall casting you, but if you list large roles that you have never played, you may not be able to measure up to your "reputation."

Open Calls

Although Equity Open Calls are limited to members of Equity, in 1988 the National Labor Relations Board required that producers hold open calls for non-union actors. These auditions can be harrowing with hundreds of actors signing up to audition for a small number of jobs.

✦ *I represent a woman who was interested in being in "Les Miz." She felt strongly that she wanted to play Cossette and although I have a twenty year relationship with the casting directors, they were disinclined to bring her in. I encouraged her to go to the open call, she did, and she got the job.*
Jim Wilhelm/DGRW

◆ *Actors' Equity surveyed 500 members and found that 47% had found jobs through open casting calls. In calls for chorus work, which has its own system, casting directors size up the hopefuls who show up and point to those who resemble the type they are seeking before holding auditions.*
Jennifer Kingson Bloom/*New York Times*[1]

Although some do get jobs in musicals through open calls, all concerned say it's an endurance contest.

◆ *It's not just wearing for the actors; the producers, directors, and casting executives also find it daunting. And only a hundred were given a chance to sing half a song and hoof a few steps. Vincent G. Liff, the casting director for "Big" and "Phantom of the Opera," who turned away no less than 250 women for "Big" alone, called the turnout frightening but said the system, while patience-trying, was valuable.*
"We have cast dozens and dozens of people through these calls," Mr. Liff said.
Jennifer Kingson Bloom/*New York Times*[2]

The most successful people in any business are smart, organized, and entrepreneurial, but almost no one starts out that way. It's like learning to walk. It takes a while before you can get your balance.

As you continue reading agents' remarks about what successful actors do, you will begin to develop an overview of the business that will help you in the process of representing yourself. It's essential to stay focused and specific, and to give up the natural urge to panic.

Bring the same creative problem-solving you use in preparing a scene to the business side of your career and you will not only be successful, you will begin to feel more in control of your own destiny.

Wrap Up

Tools for First Agent

- ✓ decent credits
- ✓ open calls
- ✓ audition tape
- ✓ stay focused
- ✓ entrepreneurial skills

4

Welcome to the Big Apple

If you've just come to the city, no matter how long you have waited to get here, you will need a period of adjustment. Don't add the stress

sources for information on temporary housing. The show business newspapers *Back Stage* and *Show Business* also offer opportunities to plug into the grapevine.

There are actor-friendly neighborhoods in the City: West Beth (downtown in the West Village) and The Manhattan Plaza (midtown on the West Side) are both artistic communities with subsidized housing and long waiting lists, but since actors are frequently out of town for jobs, sublets are available. Both of these artists' havens offer classes and are plugged into the creative forces of the city.

Areas in which rents are cheaper are the Lower East Side, below Wall Street, Chinatown, and some areas of what used to be called Hell's Kitchen in the far West 40s.

Some churches and YMCA/YWCAs have a limited amount of relatively inexpensive housing available on a temporary basis. There is also a youth hostel. For information consult the NY Convention and Visitors Bureau, Two Columbus Circle, New York, NY 10019.

There are those fabled $75 per month apartments that keep us all salivating but they have been occupied for hundreds of years by the same tenant. Don't allow yourself to keep from finding suitable housing because you are waiting for one of those fabulous deals. You don't want to use up all your good luck getting a swell apartment for 35¢. Save your luck for your big break and you'll be able to afford to pay full price.

More and more people are finding housing in Brooklyn, Queens, New Jersey and Staten Island. When I first arrived in New York, I briefly considered New Jersey (since I had children), but after much soul-searching, I realized that my dream was to come to New York City. I decided that if I was going to starve, it would be while living my dream all the way. Not everyone's dream is so particularized. There are many actors who prefer to live out of the city.

Get a Job

✦ *Keep yourself in a good state all of the time. You can't be broke. It does not work. Secure yourself a job in whatever it is that you can do, whether it be as a waiter or as a secretary, where they give you leniency to go out on auditions. Being a starving actor does not work. What works is to be healthy and to keep some money in your pocket so that you are not hysterical while you are doing this. I don't come from the point of view that you have to suffer to be an actor.*
Bruce Levy/Bruce Levy Agency

✦ *As soon as you get to town, get a survival job. You must have income. You'll need to have pictures, resumes, audition clothes, classes. You need to have money to do these things.*
Bill Timms/Peter Strain & Associates, Inc.

✦ *Before an actor begins to look for an agent, he should establish a secure foundation. He or she needs a place to live and/or a job, some friends to talk to, and pictures or at least a facsimile of pictures. It's very important that they have a comfortable place to go to during the day and be settled so they don't carry any more anxiety than necessary into an agent or manager's office.*
Some actors think an agent or a manager will turn into a surrogate mother-father-teacher-confessor. That really isn't his role. Actors get disappointed when they aren't taken care of right away. I think it's better to come in as a fully secure person so you can be sold that way. Otherwise, too much development time is wasted.
Gary Krasny/The Krasny Office

You're Only New Once

First impressions are indelible. As J. Michael Bloom (Meridian Artists/LA) puts it: "You're only new once."

✦ *You want to come to New York with training and with a base because when you meet people, the way you are at that moment is how they're going to remember you. If you meet people and you're not at your best, that's going to be the way they remember you.*

It's all those silly things your mother told you when you were growing up. You hated it, but she was right all along. Teachers do always remember you as you are the first day of class. Sometimes you can shift that image, but it's hard.
Flo Rothacker/DGRW

developing themselves and their craft. I tell all young actors: get in therapy, get into NYU, Yale, Juilliard, one of the league schools.
Jim Flynn/Jim Flynn, Inc.

✦ *I think the philosophical basis is to work as much as possible, because the more you work, the more people have an opportunity to respond to it. Everyone in this business who is not an actor makes his living by recognizing talented actors.*

The smartest thing a young playwright can do is to get to know a good, young, talented actor so that when there is a showcase of the playwright's play, he can recommend the actor. That's going to make his play look better.

There are a number of stage directors in New York that, all they can really do (to be candid), is read a script and cast well and then stay out of the way. That can often be all you need.

Casting directors, agents, playwrights, directors, even stage managers are going to remember good actors. If they want to get ahead in their business, the more they remember good actors, the better off they're gonna be. Having your work out there is the crucial thing.

Studying is important because it keeps you ready. Nobody is going to give you six weeks to get your instrument ready. It's "here's the audition; do it now," so I believe in showcases. Actors tend to be too linear in their thinking. They think, "Okay. I did this showcase and no agent came and nobody asked me to come to their office so it was a complete waste of time."

Well, I don't believe that. First of all, even a bad production is going to teach a young actor a lot of important things. Second of all, generally, if you do a good job in a play, it produces another job. Often it's in another showcase. Often, it's a year later, so if you're looking for direct links, you never see them.

What tends to happen is somebody calls you up and says, "I saw you in that show and you were terrific and would you like to come do this show?" It's like out of the blue, and it can take a long time. You may have to do eight great showcases or readings, but if your work is out there, there is an opportunity for people to get excited and if it isn't out there, then that opportunity doesn't exist. It doesn't matter how terrific you are in the office and how charming you are. None of that matters.

Tim Angle/Don Buchwald & Associates/Los Angeles

Show business takes even balanced people and chews them up and spits them out for breakfast. If you can't remain extremely focused and provide a personal life for yourself, you will have a difficult time dealing with the downs and ups of life as an actor, so either get into therapy or start meditating. Do whatever it takes to put your life in a healthy state.

✦ *There are some people I know who are brilliant actors, but I'm not willing to take responsibility for their careers because I know the rest of their life is not in order.*

Flo Rothacker/DGRW

If you are in an impossible relationship or if you have any kind of addiction problem, the business is only going to intensify it. Deal with these things first. If your life is in order, find a support group to help you keep it that way before you enter the fray.

People Who Need People

Life is easier with friends. Begin to build relationships with your peers. There are those who say you should build friendships with people who already have what you want. I understand that thinking, but it's not my idea of a good time.

It's a lot easier to live on a shoestring and/or deal with constant rejection if your friends are going through the same thing. If your friend is starring on a television show or is king of commercials and has plenty of money while you are scrambling to pay the rent, it is going to be harder to keep perspective about where you are in the process. It takes different people differing amounts of time to make the journey. Having friends who understand that will make it easier for all of you.

Ruth Gordon's seventy year career included an Oscar for acting (*Rosemary's Baby*), five Writers Guild Awards plus several Oscar nominations for screenwriting *(Pat and Mike, Inside Daisy Clover,* etc.). In her interview with Paul Rosenfield, she had words of wisdom for us all.

✦ *Life is getting through the moment. The philosopher, William James, says to "cultivate the cheerful attitude." Now nobody had more trouble than he did except me. I had more trouble in my life than anybody. But your first big trouble can be a bonanza if you live through it. Get through the first trouble, you'll probably make it through the next one.*

Children of Alcoholics), OA (Overeaters Anonymous), etc. No matter who you are, there is probably a group with which you can identify, that will provide you with confidential support for free.

You'll be better served if you don't look to these groups for your social life. They supply a forum where you can talk about what is bothering you, but these support groups are not your family and, though helpful, they are not your best friends either.

Put energy into your personal relationships to fill those needs. You create your life. Will Rogers said, "People are about as happy as they want to be." I agree, I believe we all get what we really want.

If you are a member of SAG, Equity, or AFTRA, check out their support groups or join one of their committees. You'll have the chance to be involved in a productive activity with your peers on a regular basis that will give you a family and a focus.

I prefer to see you do things that don't cost, but if you must pay for a "home away from home," check out an outfit like TVI. See page 33.

Getting to Know the City

It's easy to get around the island of Manhattan. If you are directionally challenged, this is your chance to finally understand about north, south, east, and west. The Hudson River is west and guess where the East River is?

As you travel uptown (north), the numbers get larger and as you go downtown toward Wall Street, Chinatown, and the Statue of Liberty (south), the numbers get smaller. The numbers stop at Houston (pronounced "how-ston"). Then you have to deal with street names.

The quickest way to get anywhere is on a bicycle if you have the courage. That's too scary for me, so I walk. Cabs are expensive and frequently very slow. Fastest transportation is the subway. Many people don't like it, but I've personally never had any trouble. Subways now require MetroCards which can also be used on buses. It makes sense to buy a MetroCard with many rides on it. Not only is there a discount but you won't have to stand in line each time.

You can buy MetroCards at banks and some newsstands as well as at subway stations. Some stations don't have manned token booths at all times, so plan ahead.

Go to any subway station or look in the front of the Manhattan phone book for a free subway map. You'll find addresses of New York theaters in the same place.

There are subways that only go up and down the East Side (Lexington Avenue) and some that only go up and down the West Side (7th Avenue) and some (the E & F) that do both. There are some that only go crosstown (14th Street, 42nd Street and 59th Street). Buses are great for shorter hops, but, like the subway, you must have exact change or a MetroCard.

I can walk across town in about twenty minutes; you probably can, too. Crosstown blocks go east and west and are about three times as long as downtown blocks which go north and south. It takes about the same amount of time to walk from 42nd to 59th Streets as it takes to go from Lexington Avenue to Broadway.

As I mentioned above, in the front of the phone book you'll find a guide to numbered addresses, e.g. if you are at 1501 Broadway, you are between 43rd and 44th Streets. Put that guide in the front of your appointment book, it will save you time and shoe leather.

I've included a map to give you an overview of Manhattan which includes the Broadway theater district, the Public Theater, the theater library at Lincoln Center, the TKTS Booth (half-price tickets to Broadway and off-Broadway shows), the various television networks, bookstores, etc. Here's the key:

1. ABC Television
   77 West 66th Street

2. Actors' Equity Association (AEA)
   165 West 46th Street, East of Broadway

3. Actors' Studio
   432 West 44th Street btwn 9th & 10th Avenues

   211 West 71st Street btwn Broadway & West End Avenue

7. Carnegie Hall
   881 7th Avenue at 57th Street

8. CBS Television Studios
   524 West 57th Street btwn 10th & 11th Avenues

9. City Center
   131 West 55th Street btwn 6th & 7th Avenues

10. The Drama Book Shop
    250 West 40th Street

11. HB Studios
    120 Bank Street in the Village, West of Hudson Street

12. Lincoln Center
    64th Street at Columbus Avenue

12. The Lincoln Center Library of Performing Arts
    40 Lincoln Center Plaza at 66th Street

Manhattan Street Map

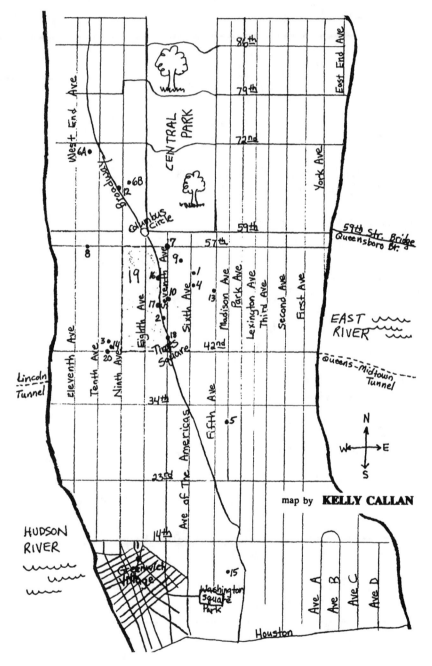

map by **KELLY CALLAN**

13. NBC Television
    30 Rockefeller Plaza at 5th Avenue & 49th Street

14. Manhattan Plaza
    43rd Street btwn 9th & 10th Avenues

15. The Public Theater
    425 Lafayette Street, at 8th Street, one block East of Broadway

42nd to 57th Streets and 6th to 9th Avenues

19. Theater Row
    42nd Street btwn 9th & 11th Avenues

The Official City Guide

Another way to get a handful of excellent Manhattan information is to pick up *The Official City Guide* available at most hotels and/or online at www.cityguideny.com. I don't think I've seen a better source of maps and information about what's going on in Manhattan. It includes useful phone numbers and a reference page detailing cross streets relative to the address. Another useful link is www.newyorkcity.com.

A Job Gives Form to Your Life

Once you have found a place to live, it is vital for more than financial reasons to find a job.

Having a job gives form to your life, gives you a place to go every day, a family of people to relate to, and helps you feel as though you are part of the City and not just a tourist.

Nothing feeds depression more than sitting at home alone in a strange city. Even if you know your way around, you'll find that as time goes on, activity is the friend of the actor. Depression feeds on itself and must not be allowed to get out of hand.

If you are fortunate and tenacious enough to find a job in the business, you'll find you are not only finally in the system on some level, but that you're being paid to continue your education. There is no way in the world you can learn what it's really like to be in the business until you experience it firsthand. You'll get to spend every day with people who are interested in the same things you are. Who knows? You might not even like show business when you get a closer look. Better to find out now.

Casting Society of America Job File

Sitting in an agent's office waiting for an appointment, I met a young actor who was manning the phones. He told me he has worked as a casting assistant in both Los Angeles and New York and had come to his present job by faxing his resume to the Casting Society of America job file.

The pay is small, but as he pointed out, the access to the business was well worth it. He said he wouldn't trade the higher salary for the business maturity he had acquired.

Casting Society of America
2565 Broadway #185
New York, NY 10025
212-868-1260 Ext. 22
e-mail: castsoc@earthlink.net
www.castingsociety.com

I visited the CSA's website recently and found an option to send a virtual postcard to casting directors inviting them to showcases, screenings, comedy appearances, etc. You can also search for a particular casting director's name although, unfortunately, there is no formal list of all the casting directors.

✦ *If you can combine a showbiz job with flexible hours permitting auditions, that's the best of all possibilities. Always be available. Don't say you are an actor if you have a 9-to-5 job. If you must waitress, do it at night.*
Sharon Carry/Carry Company

As soon as you are working in the business in any category, you are in the system and on your way. I don't want to imply that coming up with one of these jobs is the easiest task in the world, but it is definitely worth the effort.

Encountering Agents

Before your resume is ready for you to be interviewing agents as

Get Into an Acting Class

In order to find a good teacher, you'll have to do some research. Who did he study with? What is the caliber of his students? Has this person worked professionally? You want someone whose advice is not theoretical. Work in class is totally different from actual professional work.

No one can teach you to act; a teacher can only stimulate your imagination and focus your work. Not everyone will be able to do that for you. Look for the teacher that will.

✦ *Audit classes. See the atmosphere of the class. If it seems to be an environment to stimulate healthy growth in you, then check out the technique, for technique is only part of it. Be sure you are going to be in a creative space, then you find out about the technique. Is this the place where I can expand? Is this a place where I can fall on my face, where they will support me in picking myself up?*
Bruce Levy/Bruce Levy Agency

✦ *Like anything else that you're going to invest money and time in, an actor should shop around and see what's best for him. See someone whose work you admire and find out who they study with and audit that class.*
Jerry Kahn/Jerry Kahn, Inc.

✦ *Choose an acting class that keeps expanding you, not just your acting, but your creativity and your being. You need constant expansion. If you are not getting that or if you feel closed down, don't continue. If you feel closed down in class, that's happening to your audition, also.*

Bruce Levy/Bruce Levy Agency

Teachers

✦ *Actors should study with many different teachers and take what they need from all the different approaches.*

Meg Pantera/Meg Pantera, The Agency

Here is a list of well-regarded teachers in New York. Some I know personally, some are recommended by agents or actors whose judgment I trust.

William Esper is a widely respected acting teacher and director who has headed his own studio in NYC for over thirty-five years and continues as director of the Professional Actor Training Programs at Mason Gross School of the Arts at Rutgers University.

A graduate of the Neighborhood Playhouse School of Theater, Esper trained as an actor and teacher with mentor, Sanford Meisner, with whom he worked closely as a teacher and director for fifteen years.

Esper charges $300 a month for three-hour classes that meet twice a week. Classes run September through June with a six-week Summer Intensive. There are many teaching associates at his studio and prices vary with the teacher. All teachers have had extensive teacher training with Mr. Esper.

The studio also offers classes in Voice & Speech, Mask, Movement, Shakespeare, and Script Analysis; as well as workshops in Cold Reading, Auditioning and On-Camera Technique.

Esper's list of amazing credits is lengthy and includes a juicy list of students from William Hurt to John Malkovich and is featured on his web page, www.esperstudio.com. Call 212-904-1350 for information..

I studied at *HB Studios* when I first came to New York. HB continues not only to be a rich resource for excellent teachers who are all working, but offers classes that are extremely reasonable.

You are allowed to audit any class once for $7 and they encourage you to audit many classes in order to find the one that is right for you. There is a $45 registration fee and the classes average out to be about

$10 each depending on the teacher and the class.

Musical classes cost more because there is an accompanist. If you check the web page and pick any teacher and click on the right menu, you'll get class times, how many classes there are, how much it costs, and the teacher's background.

Until I checked the web page, I was unaware that HB offers a full array of classes and that full-time students can pursue classes six days a week and end up with a conservatory education. Whether you are

rehearse or how to do it. So they just end up memorizing lines and hoping a director will move them around. And whether it's for the camera or a live audience, you need to know what to work on at home alone like a musician, like a painter, like a writer."

Ten years ago at UCLA, feeling that women's stories were under-represented in the media, Karen created Women on the Edge to encourage women to write and perform their own stories. After fourteen weeks, the actor performs a ten-minute piece, which may lead to a screenplay, a play, or a one-woman show. 212-243-7570.

Karen also teaches Acting for Directors to second year students at NYU Film School. For requirements, check NYU Tisch School of the Arts/Film Department. All Karen's classes require an audition for entrance.

Karen is one of the producers of *Uta Hagen's Acting Class Video*. Though no substitute for a class with Miss Hagen, the video is still an amazing teaching tool. It's available at www.utahagenvideo.com for $49.95.

Jacqueline Segal charges $150 monthly for four two-hour classes and gets $100 hourly for private coaching. She also conducts a one-day workshop, Onstage/Offstage, for actors and non-actors using the tools of acting as tools for living more freely both offstage and on. $150. 212-683-9428.

Terry Shreiber Studios charge $190-$220 monthly for a weekly class that runs from five-to-six hours. TSS has an amazing staff including veteran *One Life to Live* director, Peter Miner, who now teaches film direction at the Columbia University Graduate Film School, and Tony Award winning actress Betty Buckley. Prices vary so check the website for information on the school, classes, teachers, etc. http://t-s-s.org or call 212-741-0209.

Acting classes at *The Independent School of Acting* are taught by *Greg Zittel*. The twice weekly two-to-three hour classes runs $250. New classes are constantly forming. Zittel says the classes provide an atmosphere where a student can grow both as a person and as an actor. Classes meets twice weekly on the stage. Camera work is done in the film studio when appropriate. The web page is www.theindependent.org. For an interview call or e-mail Greg: 212-929-6192 or Greg49@aol.com.

Jessica Lange, Harvey Keitel, Laura Dern and Meg Ryan are just a few of the actors *Greta Seacat* coaches. Her package of eight-to-ten classes that run four-to-five hours is $565. She teaches all over the world. 212-564-9286.

Respected Los Angeles actor-director-author *Allan Miller* comes to New York a few times a year for weekend classes. He teaches several five-hour classes for $75 each. There are discounts if you take more than one class. Check out his excellent book, *A Passion for Acting*, to see if he appeals to you. Allan.Miller@sbcglobal.net or 818-907-6262.

Improv guru *Gary Austin* (one of the founders of The Groundlings) also teaches all over the country. His classes range from Improv Technique to Characters to Acting Technique/Making Choices. He works with students on an ongoing basis to create their own material. Classes have different prices relative to content and time but average about $25 hourly. Details at www.garyaustin.org or call 800-DOG-TOES.

All price quotes are current, but confirm rates when you call.

If I have mentioned a studio with many teachers, know that all teachers are not equal. Hang out a little to see who the students are and audit to find the teacher who seems right for you. See at least three for comparison. In a good class, you'll learn as much about yourself and the marketplace as you will about acting.

If you're broke, see if you can work in exchange for tuition.

Showcases

Showcases offer visibility, experience and the ability to hone the most important skill of all: getting along with people. But choose your material carefully. Playing *King Lear* may give you great satisfaction and stretch you as an actor, but it doesn't present you in a castable light for anything other than a Shakespearean company.

+ *I think they should try to find a showcase which presents them in a castable light, in a role that's appropriate, and that is convenient for agents to get to. You can't get me to go to Brooklyn.*

Before inviting agents, they should consider (and perhaps have professional advice) whether or not the project is worth inviting agent to. You can engender hostility wasting an agent's evening if it's abominable.

TVI

Gee, how to write about TVI without looking like I'm on their payroll? At first glance, TVI looks like one of those places I tell actors to stay away from. They offer classes, casting director workshops, advice, and they charge a membership fee. They've got pictures from a cross-section of photographers in their waiting room, making it look like they might get kickbacks. They want to be your mother offering a home away from home.

Now, having visited TVI, I cannot think of a single bad thing to say. It is a club for actors. TVI provides computers, help texturing your resume (they'll even keep it in their computer and update it for you at no charge), free industry mailing labels, rehearsal space, a research gallery of photographers' work (no kickbacks), a place to hang out with fellow actors, and various other perks.

Started in New York in 1986 by ex-Cunningham, Escott & Dipene commercial agent Alan S. Nusbaum, and joined soon after by his wife and partner Deborah Koffler, the organization has thrived because the goal has been not only to teach business skills to actors, but to help them translate those skills into jobs by providing access to all the necessary tools.

The annual membership fee is $450 (about $38 a month) payable in two installments. Each year of membership costs less and by the fourth year becomes $150 annually. Classes cost extra but are discounted for members.

While waiting to meet with Nusbaum, I encountered an actor at the bulletin board who said he was a former member. I asked if he had had a good experience. He was unhappy because none of the casting director workshops resulted in a job or an interview. I'm not a fan of casting director workshops because I think casting directors should see you for free. I asked Alan about the actor's complaints.

Alan told me (and I saw all the posted disclaimers) that TVI makes clear that the workshops are opportunities to ask industry professions questions about the casting process and that no casting is involved.

Hope springs eternal, though. No matter how many times anyone tells that to an actor, in the actor's heart of hearts he secretly thinks that the act of being in the presence of CD, agent, or director, is going to result in stardom — or, at the very least, an audition.

TVI isn't going to get you any work, but their club/family atmosphere might help you feel less isolated. It will definitely give you access to other people in the business and upgrade your business skills in a protected environment created by someone who actually worked successfully in the business. TVI is a business, yes, but it also appears to me to really have the actor's best interests at heart.

I've only had contact with the Los Angeles branch, but I'm sure the New York branch must be as trustworthy.

TVI Actors Studio
165 W 46th Street, #509
New York, NY 10036
212-784-6500
www.tvistudios.com

Before You Come to New York: The Connected Theater Schools

I was a first generation college student, lucky that my family sent me to any school. Though I yearned for a school I had read about, I had no understanding of the importance of a theater pedigree from the right school or I might have found a way to attend.

If you are preparing to study, consider a connected school. Some schools are not only significantly superior to others, but there is a group of schools universally accepted as the most comprehensive training for young actors and whose cachet instantly alerts the antennae of buyers (CDs, agents, producers, directors, etc.). This is where the creme de la creme of new young actors, the next Meryl Streep or Paul Newman, are coming from.

These schools were members of a collective referred to as "the leagues." Though that collective no longer exists, "leagues" has become a handle for the prestigious schools of the moment though I generally refer to them as "connected."

They all have web pages. Some are more user friendly than others, so be patient. Whether or not a school should be included in the list

. . . . program . . . . Cincinnati Conservatory of Music and the Boston Conservatory of Music. Each year, these schools' industry showcases attract almost every agent and casting director in New York City. Their graduates probably have the highest employment percentage of ANY drama school, musical or otherwise, graduate or undergraduate.

Juilliard is, of course, one of the two or three best drama programs in the country, but does not specialize in musicals. Nonetheless many Broadway musical stars have gotten their start there, including Patti LuPone and Kevin Kline.

A number of other schools offer good programs as well, although they lack the prestige of the above mentioned three: Carnegie Mellon, Northwestern, and, to a lesser extent, Michigan and NYU. Questions you need to ask are:

Does it offer a Bachelor of Fine Arts or a Bachelor of Arts degree? Aim for the BFA, as that's the sign of an actual professional training program. Does it offer a showcase in NYC or LA? There's little point investing in a degree if the industry doesn't see you at the end of it. What sort of performance options do you have? How recently have the faculty actually been participating in the biz?

A note of caution to close. Remember that everyone auditioning for these programs has been the star of their schools. Stature at your high school rarely guarantees success beyond. However, don't be intimidated by a lackluster resume either. What gets people into these schools is their audition and their look, and nothing else will really matter.

Andy Lawler

The Other Cool Schools

In addition to those schools, here is a list of other schools, based on hearsay and research that are thought to be the chosen schools at this moment in time. The best way to judge is to check out the curriculum as well as the track record of graduates via their web pages.

American Conservatory Theater, Carey Perloff
30 Grant Avenue, 6th Floor
San Francisco, CA 94108
415-834-3200
www.act-sfbay.org/conservatory/index.html

Carnegie Mellon, Drama Department/Elizabeth Bradley
College of Fine Arts/School of Drama
5000 Forbes Avenue, Room #108
Pittsburgh, PA 15213
412-268-2392
www.cmu.edu/cfa/drama

Columbia University in the City of New York, Kristin Linklater
305 Dodge Hall, Mail Code 1808
2960 Broadway
New York, NY 10027-6902
212-854-2875
www.columbia.edu/cu/arts

Harvard University, Richard Orchard
American Repertory Theater/Loeb Drama Center
64 Brattle Street
Cambridge, MA 02138
617-495-2668
www.amrep.org

Juilliard School, Kathy Hood, Director of Admissions
60 Lincoln Center Plaza
New York, NY 10023
212-799-5000 Ext. 4
www.juilliard.edu/splash.html

New York University/Drama Department
Arthur Bartow, Artistic Director
721 Broadway, 3rd Floor
New York, NY 10003
212-998-1850
www.nyu.edu/tisch

North Carolina School of the Arts, Gerald Freedman

847-491-7023
www.communication.northwestern.edu

State University of New York (at Purchase), Dean Irby
735 Anderson Hill Road
Purchase, NY 10577
914-251-6360
http://www.purchase.edu/academics/taf

Yale School of Drama, Yale University, Lloyd Richards
Post Office Box 208325
New Haven, CT 06520-8325
203-432-1505
www.yale.edu/drama

If you graduate from one of these schools, you are immediately thought to be the creme de la creme as far as NYC/LA are concerned. You probably will be better trained. Actors in these programs are courted by agents and some procure representation as early as freshman year. The career boost by the annual showcase of graduating students, produced specifically for an audience of agents and casting directors in New York and Los Angeles, is priceless.

◆ *Although the leagues may sometimes lead to auditions for immediate employment on a soap opera, in summer stock, in an off-Broadway play, more often it serves as*

a casting director's mental Rolodex of actors to use in future projects.
Jill Gerston, *New York Times*[4]

All of the league schools offer excellent training, but they are hard to get into and expensive, so consider carefully and have a backup. This type of education requires a big commitment of time and money. Choose the school that is right for you.

Even if you are educated at the best schools and arrive highly touted with interest from agents, ex-William Morris agent Joanna Ross told me there is still a period of adjustment.

✦ *When you come out of school, you gotta freak out for a while. Actors in high-powered training programs working night and day doing seven different things at once get out of school and suddenly there is no demand for their energy. It takes a year, at least, to learn to be unemployed. And they have to learn to deal with that. It happens to everybody. It's not just you.*
Joanna Ross

Even if you can't make it to a league school, all is not lost.

✦ *The truth is, a great performance in the leagues can jump-start a career, but if these kids have talent, they'll get noticed. They just won't be as fast out of the starting gate...they just have to do it the old-fashioned way by pounding the pavements, reading "Back Stage," calling up friends, going to see directors they know and knocking on agents' doors.*
Jill Gerston, *New York Times*[5]

Market Research

Analyzing the marketplace and using that information wisely can save you years of unfocused activity. If you were starting any other kind of business, you would expect to do extensive research to see if there was a need for the product you had decided to sell. In addition to checking out actors, note who is working and where, and keep a file on CDs, producers, directors, and writers.

Note which writers are writing parts for people like you. Learn and practice remembering the names of everybody. Know who the critics are. Note those whose taste agrees with yours. Think of this educational process as your Ph.D.

If you want to be a force in the business, begin to think of yourself as such and assume your rightful place. Synonyms of the word "force" inspire me: "Energy, power, strength, vigor, vitality, impact, value, weight."

With each new detail about the business that you ingest and have ready at your fingertips, your vitality increases. With each play you read, see, rehearse, perform in and with each writer, actor, director, CD, costumer, etc. that you support, your power grows.

The Unions

_____ .. .. give you a chance to sharpen your acting tools.

Becoming a member of the union is a worthy goal. I can remember the thrill when I got my Equity card (somehow that was the card that meant you were an actor), but I was far along in my resume before I joined. It makes sense to wait.

Working as an Extra

While work as an extra gives you the opportunity to be on the set, unless you are looking for more extra work I would not list it on the resume. You want any agent, producer or casting director thinking of you for principal parts, so don't cloud his vision.

✦ _Working as an extra could be valuable for someone who has never been on a set. Working on a soap can help you become familiar with cameras and absorb information. It's not something that should be on your resume or even brought up to the agent._
Flo Rothacker/DGRW

There are specific directors or producers for whom you might make an exception.

✦ _An extra job on a Woody Allen film could turn out to be a good job because Woody sometimes notices extras, gives them lines and you can end up working for_

weeks. You could end up getting upgraded or if you got a chance to work on a Sydney Lumet film as an extra, think of what you could learn.
Marvin Josephson/Gilla Roos, Ltd.

If you plan to be a career extra, working as an extra makes sense. If your goal is to play principal parts, why amass a resume that advertises you in a different capacity? It's tempting to accept extra work to qualify for guild membership, pay rent, keep insurance active or get on a set. I understand that. So saying, the quote below speaks for itself.

I asked the agent if he had "John Smith" work as an extra, wouldn't casting directors and producers now only consider John to be an extra?

✦ *We all do. I spoke to a casting director the other day about an actor and that's exactly what she said. The actor has to learn where to draw the line and say, "Okay, I can't do this anymore."*
Anonymous Agent

A lot of people can't. They get used to the money and the insurance and their resumes reflect that they are full-time extras. This otherwise credible agent encourages actors to work as extras (after all, he is making a commission), expecting them to know when to draw the line at what is too much extra work.

To me it's like saying, "Here, these drugs will make you feel better. Just take them for a while, I know you will be able to stop in time." If you are not ready to get work as a principal on a regular basis, it may not be time for you to be in the union.

It would be a lot more advantageous for you to work in some other capacity in order to pay your rent or observe the business from the inside. Become an assistant or work in production. You will see what goes on, make some money and you won't be fooling yourself into thinking you are really acting. You will be more driven to pursue work that will further your career.

Emergencies

SAG, Equity, and AFTRA all have financial assistance available to members in an emergency situation. If you are not a member of a union, ask your acting teacher for advice.

There are also many city agencies equipped to deal with people in need. There is low-cost counseling available through the city of New

York and through the schools of psychology of some un
the schools or look in the front of the white pages of the
for information.

Invaluable Trade Papers/The Trades

Ross Reports Television & Film (*Ross Report*) is a monthly publicati
that prints contact information on agents, casting dir...

ᵍ--- ᴅⁱʳᵉᶜᵗᵒʳʸ, etc.
A single copy costs $6.95 on newsstands with a year's subscription
(10 issues) going for $59. The magazine is available at The Drama Book
Shop and most good newsstands as well as directly from the publisher.
RR also publishes stand-alone books: *Film Casting & Production Directory,
Television Commercial Casting & Production Directory*, and other guides.

In the last edition of *The New York Agent Book*, I reported that
RRT&F was in the process of creating its own website with a projected
launch date of summer 2001, but since it's already 2004 and there's no
website, I wouldn't hold my breath.

If you type in www.rossreports.com all you get is *Back Stage* and an ad for
RRT&F since both publications are owned by the same publisher.

Ross Reports Television & Film
770 Broadway
New York, NY 10003
800-817-3273
www.backstage.com/backstage/rossreports/index.jsp
e-mail: rossreports@rossreports.com

Back Stage and *Show Business* are New York's weekly showbiz
newspapers ("trades") and rich resources of casting information for
non-union and union theater, film and television.

Both newspapers state that they have not checked the veracity of the
ads and suggest caution and skepticism. Some ads will be scams but

New York's premier actor reference guide is now partnered with the venerable Breakdown Service, *Players Guide*. Published in January to take advantage of pilot season, membership in the annual directory includes listings in two online casting resources, the Academy of Motion Picture Arts & Sciences produced *Academy Players Directory*, and *PG's* own version of the book.

Members are also eligible for electronic submission by their agent or manager through The Link or Star Caster online submission systems. Inclusion in the *Guide* is now thought of as a membership and a card entitling members to discounts for a variety of actor-friendly services like photographers, vocal coaches, etc. is part of the package.

The *Guide* is routinely used by casting directors, agents, and producers to jog their memories, check for actor's agent affiliation and/or find a new face, and is a potent tool for actors who are already in the union or who have agency representation. The fee is $98 for the first listing for one picture in one category.

For an additional charge, you can add up to three pictures, include your full resume and feature yourself in additional categories. *PG* now has categories for children and stunt performers.

Players Guide
123 W 44th Street, 2J
New York, NY 10036
212-302-9474
www.playersguideny.com

Get on the mailing list for the next *Guide*. You will have to sign a legal document saying you are in one of the performer unions. This is not something to lie about since casting directors consult the guide looking for union actors. If a casting director calls you from the book and you are not in the union, you could be sued, but if you are a member of the union and ready to book, you should be listed.

Stumbling and Physics

You're not going to be perfect

Wrap Up

Personal Resources

✓ support group
✓ family teachers

Geographical Resources

✓ phone books
✓ maps
✓ NYC Convention Bureau

Professional Resources

✓ job in business
✓ acting class/teachers
✓ theatrical publications
✓ three-year stumble rule

5
Self-Knowledge

Before you can sell yourself to an agent or the marketplace, you've got to figure out what you have to sell. Recently I got an e-mail from a reader who told me that she sent her picture and resume to many agents. Many agents asked to meet her, but no one would sign her. I asked her to send me her picture. She was an adorable sunny Sally Field type. I could understand why everyone had wanted to meet her.

I studied the pictures trying to figure out why all these agents passed after asking to meet her. I wondered what didn't match. Finally I wrote asking if by chance she had an "edge." When she answered affirmatively, I knew we had identified the problem. All the agents who asked to see her obviously had room on their lists for Sally Field but not for Angelina Jolie. Once the actress adjusted the picture to match her personality, she was quickly signed.

You absolutely must be able to see yourself with a clear eye to find out which one you are and package yourself accordingly.

✦ *[Actors need to] be aware of their strongest gift and concentrate on it.*
Diana Doussant/HWA Talent Representatives

✦ *Before you start meeting people, you need to find an image to present. Check to see what the demand is and where you fit in.*
Ann Steele/Ann Steele Agency

✦ *Know yourself. Know what you want to do.*
Archer King/Archer King, Ltd.

✦ *Be the best person you can be. Learn about yourself. You need a solid center to deal with life when things get tough. You have to know what your bottom line is and what you are willing to sacrifice in order to get what you want.*
Jack Menasche/Carlson-Menasche

✦ *Know yourself. You are the president of your company and you are the product. If you know what you've got, you can market the product better.*
Bill Timms/Peter Strain & Associates, Inc.

If you don't have any insights into your persona yet, acting class is a good place to start your investigation. Your teacher will probably

When people use the word talent in relation to actors, they usually refer to acting talent, but other talents govern how effective the acting talent can be. Once you reach a certain level, all your competition is terrific. Any one actor sitting in the waiting room would be a good choice, but the talent to self-motivate, focus, and maintain balance and cool under pressure will be the deciding factor in who prevails.

◆ *Talent has never been enough. Talent never will be enough. You have to have commitment and a singular purpose. Every decision has to be a career decision.*
Archer King/Archer King, Ltd.

When you hear about the thousands of starving actors vying for five agents and one part, you can screen out many of those thousands. They won't be your competition because they have no appetite for taking care of business. It doesn't matter if there are only five agents and one part as long as you get the part and one of the agents.

I asked agents to name the most important single piece of advice they would like to give to actors. Almost everyone gave some version of the same answer.

Know Which One You Are

Don't expect to play Catherine Zeta-Jones' parts if you look like Bonnie Hunt. When I first arrived in New York, I did everything I could lest I be mistaken for the middle-class lady from Texas I was. I wanted to be a sophisticated New Yorker.

What I didn't realize, Texas accent not withstanding, was that my very middle-classness is what I had to sell. I have played women who went to Vassar, but more often buyers can and will get someone for those parts who actually went to Vassar.

I'm an authentic lady from Texas who has raised three children and had various life experiences that continue informing my persona. I'm a mother, a carpenter, a quilter, a theme partygiver, an ex-Catholic, a grandmother and on and on.

There is nobody else who has my particular components. If I don't prize what is uniquely me and find a way to tie that to a universality of the life experience, not only will I not work consistently and honestly, but my life will be a mess as well.

Also, as a person who has just begun to travel, I cannot say strongly enough how I wish I had started sooner. Traveling piques the curiosity and gives you a much broader life perspective.

✦ *I personally believe that anyone who comes into this business has one point where they can enter the business: literally a skill, a qualification, that will get them a job tomorrow.*

If they are willing to take the time to find out what it is and go for that area, they can get hired, they can start working. And then they can begin to explore the other areas that they might not yet be prepared for.

There are certain qualifications that are required in every area. People who want to do musical theater have to be able to sing and dance. They need to take the classes. They must do regional theater and work their way up, just like in corporate America. Those who want to do film and TV, other than those soap beauties who land a job just on their looks, you have to have certain qualifications.

Whatever area you are strongest in, you should go for that first. Then when you are making money in the business, you interview better and you audition better. You meet people better when you are working in the business than when you are a waiter or a waitress trying to get just any job. You're going for film, you're going for commercials, you're going for television, and just grabbing for everything rather than learning to focus and say, "Where can I get hired today?"

Once you are working in the business, then you can move your way through the path you want to be on. That's the client I like to work with. One that is already at this point and we can move you from here to here to here and take you to where you want to be. Then you are a goal-oriented career-driven client.

H. Shep Pamplin/Agents for the Arts

✦ *Actors need to be in touch with who they are, their type, their limitations, their strengths, their weaknesses. They have an inability to grasp the fact that they can't be seen for everything in town and that just because a friend gets an appointment doesn't mean he will get one too. Actors have to figure out what they are right for and what they are best at; they need to know their own limitations.*
Gary Krasny/The Krasny Office

✦ *Know your place in the business. It's good to have goals and expectations but*

actor's career is over unless they have a good solid foundation of training.
Jim Flynn/Jim Flynn, Inc.

✦ *A lot of people are just totally unrealistic. They're either young and unattractive and/or overweight, and inexperienced. And they do have a chance of being an actor, but when you look like that, it's not going to happen for twenty or twenty-five years. They'll have to be a character person. They have a fantasy of acting and they haven't done anything about it. They must do the work, they must learn the craft.*
Lionel Larner/Lionel Larner Ltd.

✦ *An actor can develop objectivity. It's very difficult. I don't know how one does it, but one has to have a certain objectivity about oneself and not freak out in certain situations that are difficult; in a crisis, not to allow your emotional life to carry you over into decisions that are not correct decisions. Decisions have to be weighed over a period of time and not in hysteria.*
Jeff Hunter/William Morris Agency

✦ *Realistically, they've got to really look. If they want to be on a soap, they should know there are requirements to being on a soap. Training. Training and a certain look. Each soap has a different style and a different look. Someone says, "I want to be on a soap" and I say, "Which one?" and the actor doesn't know what they are or what soap hires what kind of person. Actors have to do their homework.*
William Schill/William Schill Agency

A friend of mine struggled when she first came to Los Angeles. I tried to help her by suggesting a part in a show I was doing. Mary was a young pretty actress with great comic gifts. The part was the town bad girl. She said, "You obviously don't know who I am. I have no breasts. No one will ever cast me in a part like that."

She wasn't whining, just stating a fact. When she got her break, it was playing an upper crust young lady born with a silver spoon in her mouth. The clarity with which she was able to see herself gave her a focus on and offstage that won her huge rewards. She became a hugely successful actress.

It's Your Machine

In an interview for *Back Stage West,* Sigourney Weaver quoted George Wolfe's speech to graduates of NYU's Tisch School for the Arts.

✦ *He said early on he'd written this musical called "Paradise" and he'd had great hopes for it. And the day it opened was the day it closed. He looked out at all the students and said, "I'm going to tell you what your greatest teacher is, and the greatest creative tool you have in your career. It's failure. Failure will teach you all these things that you need to know."*

He said, "It's like standing in a huge casino and everyone has a slot machine. And you're feeding your slot machine and nothing is happening and all around you people are hitting the jackpot and getting all this stuff. And you're going, 'Well, I want to go over there to that machine. It's obviously a better machine than mine.' "But," he said, "Stick with your own machine. It may take you longer. But when you hit, you're still yourself."

Scott Poudfit, *Back Stage West*

✦ *Actors make a big mistake when they turn over their power to everybody else, making it about everybody else. Actors have to be very clear about who they are and what choices they are going to make when they go into auditions, and, if it's not working, to change their direction. You can't blame it on everybody else.*

Actors don't understand how the business works. I can't really blame them. All they want to do is act and everything seems to get in the way of doing their piece. I feel bad about that. They don't understand the reality of what it takes to mount a project, the amount of money involved, the fact that everybody involved is scared to death for their lives, their reputations, and that when somebody comes walking through the door, they better be less scared than these people are or they're not going

to get the job. Nobody's going to trust them with the money and the responsibilities that go with some of the roles.
Marvin Starkman/Producer

Sometimes we do get the idea that insecurity is charming and that admitting it is even endearing. We announce to buyers at an audition that we are petrified of being there and that we are sure we won't do our best.

If you enjoy being a basket case, take responsibility for that. This can be a marketable attribute if you prepare yourself to play those kinds of roles. Otherwise, get yourself together and start behaving as though you have complete confidence in your abilities. Pretty soon, you won't be pretending anymore.

All we have is now. If you are not fulfilled by the now, get out of the business. If the payoff for you is the big bucks, the Tony, the Oscar or the Emmy, change jobs now. You will miss your whole life waiting for the prize. If you are unlucky enough to get the prize with this mindset, you will find you are still the same unhappy person that you were the day before, but now you have an Oscar.

Mental health, balance and self-esteem are essential.

✦ *An actor is in a very tough position because he has to believe in himself in order to produce. On the other hand, there's a point where an actor believes so much in himself that he's unrealistic. There's a dichotomy between self-confidence and self-infatuation.*
Jeff Hunter/William Morris Agency

✦ *Don't take it personally. If you don't get a job, that's not indicative of how good you were. There are so many things that come into play: age, size, coloring, if the voice quality didn't make the match they were looking for with other voice qualities, and on and on and on. You could be the best at the job and still not get it. Some actors are crushed. They know they did a brilliant job.*

I hear from the CD that the actor did a brilliant job and didn't get it. An actor has to have resiliency. It's a hard thing to have. He has to do a lot of work on himself personally. In order to be a good actor, you must keep yourself vulnerable and if you are vulnerable, you will take it personally.

You must get off it, go away from it, move on to the next thing. Be crushed and get on with it. If you carry it forward, you will be pulled under.
Bruce Levy/Bruce Levy Agency

The late Barry Douglas from DGRW was articulate in his analysis of the actor's self-confidence.

✦ *The most important person to like you is the audience. Before the audience can like you, the producer has to agree to pay your salary. Before the producer agrees to pay your salary, the director has to agree to work with you.*

Before the director can agree to work with you, odds are, the casting director has to bring you in and say you're right for the role. Before the casting director can say you're right for the role, an agent has to submit you. Before any of these people get to see you, the first person who has to say, "I'm good," is the actor.

You've got to be confident enough to take a risk with a piece of material, to look at a piece and say, "Ah, I can expose the humanity of this character; I can develop the creativity of this moment of the theater or film or television better than anyone in the universe. I am the first person on this." If the actor doesn't believe that, no one else will. It's got to come from the actor first. The actor who is too insecure to ask for an agent just might not make it.
Barry Douglas

Reality

In a fantasy business, it's a constant struggle to maintain perspective and remain excruciatingly realistic.

✦ *Realize that everybody's career is different. Someone may be twenty-five years old and be a star and then another actor may not make a dime until they are fifty. Actors have to relax and not be so concerned with success. You have to be a constant actor. You can't say, "Well, my friend is doing a Long Wharf show and I'm just doing off-Broadway." Everybody's career is different.*
Harry Packwood/Harry Packwood Talent

✦ *It's a business of survival. Your turn will come if you're good. It may not come as often as it should, but it'll come. They will eventually find you. You can make it if you can survive and you can only survive if you have no choice.*

Some go into the business saying, "Well, I'll do this for five years and I'll see what it's like or I'll do something else." If you have something else you can happily do, do it. It's only the people who are so committed, so desperate in some way that they'll put up with the humiliation, that they will allow themselves on ten minutes notice to be there, they'll allow themselves to be open and vulnerable; to still expose who they are and still be strong and protected enough to survive that kind of open wound life, they're the only ones who are going to make it, the people who have no choice.

own path. It may not be the path you want, but in the end it's better for you.
Scott Poudfit, *Back Stage West*[7]

✦ *This is a business that rightfully or wrongfully, prefers prettier people. The prettier person gets the second look. It's a reflection of what the audience wants.*
Tim Angle/Don Buchwald & Associates/Los Angeles

✦ *I believe you will arrive at the success point you are intended to arrive at simply by working hard, not faltering, and having confidence that it does happen. It does happen. You get where you're supposed to get in our business.*
Fifi Oscard/Fifi Oscard Agency, Inc.

✦ *Just because you don't get the job doesn't mean you're not good. There are many variables that you have no control over. An actor commits to a difficult life. He can't get a job and expect to be employed for five years like other people are. That is not an actor's life.*
Bruce Levy/Bruce Levy Agency

✦ *Don't look at other actors' careers from the wrong end of the telescope. Don't look at what they did and think, "Oh, they just went from one thing to the next. It was just this inevitable golden path and they just had to walk along it."*
Tim Angle/Don Buchwald & Associates/Los Angeles

While you are paying your dues, you might get a job that gives you visibility and money for a month or even a year or two that makes you think you are further along in the process than you are.

Once your series (only one job, after all, no matter how long it lasts) or movie or play is over, you are not visible in that show business way. You may think your career is over just because employment opportunities are no longer so high profile.

Visibility is a double-edged sword. In television especially, the buyer may prefer a talented new face over an actor who has just finished a series. Frequently a semi-famous face finds itself unemployed because the buyer thinks it's too identifiable with a previous show.

Consistent Work

The task that takes more time than anything else is looking for and winning the work. Even two-time Academy Award winner Sally Field says it isn't like she thought it would be. She's constantly reading scripts, looking for things. Then, when there is something wonderful to do, she still has lots of competitors.

That's depressing, isn't it? It never lets up. I think sometimes that if they just gave me all the jobs, that I might lose interest and leave the business. I certainly wouldn't mind putting that one to the test.

Assess Yourself & the Marketplace

Begin to actively assess which one you are. Are you a young character person? A juvenile? Someone who is right for a soap? In order to see yourself clearly within the framework of the business, study the marketplace. View theater, television, and film with distance. Notice what kinds of actors consistently work. What is common to the people that work? Notice who is like you and who is not. Keep a list of roles you have seen that you realistically think you would have been right for. Ask your agent if he agrees.

As you become informed about the business, you will begin to perceive the essence of people and notice its role in the casting process. More important than the look is essence. The thing that is the same in the many diverse roles of Robert De Niro is the strength of spirit.

Practice thinking like a casting director. Identify the essence of Kevin Kline, Billy Crystal, and Whoopi Goldberg. Cast them in other people's roles. What would have been the effect if Tom Cruise had played Russell Crowe's part in *Gladiator*? What if Gwyneth Paltrow had played Julia Roberts' role in *Erin Brockovich*? Impossible? Yes, but this exercise will help you understand why you will never be cast in certain roles and why no one else should be cast in your parts — once you figure out what those parts are.

Does your appearance match your essence? Another responsibility you have is to be the best looking you that you can be, given what you came with. As Tim Angle said, the business gravitates toward prettier people. Just as in life. Getting upset about that fact is like throwing

"We'll make our own luck." I got courage because I was five-foot-nothing and not showgirl-beautiful. Very few beauties are great actresses.
Paul Rosenfield, *Los Angeles Times*[8]

The Process

✦ *Nobody changes the rules. What you can do is play the game for what you want or at least toward your ends. Nobody will force you to do work that you find insulting or demeaning. You have to figure out the rules in order to figure out how to play the game. You have to figure out what is a variable and what's not.*

If actors would take the time to put themselves in the shoes of the people they're dealing with, they would very quickly figure out what's reasonable and what's not. Actors don't understand why Equity Principal Auditions are a bad idea.

The reason is that no one can look at 250 people auditioning in a single day and give an accurate response. That's one of the reasons they only see forty people for a role. Knowing that isn't going to make your life easier, but it means it's not some arbitrary system where God touches this person and says, "You get to audition," and you, as the untouched person, sit there wondering. If you think about a director casting a play and you understand what he has to do to cast it as well as possible, at least you know what you're up against. It's not some vague, amorphous obstacle. It's not fair but at least it makes sense.

What you know is never as bad as your imagination. If you know what you're up against, it can be difficult, but at least it's concrete. What you don't know, your imagination turns into, "Everyone in the business knows I shouldn't be doing this.

I'm just not talented." It's like conspiracy theories.
Tim Angle/Don Buchwald & Associates/Los Angeles

When Sigourney Weaver was a young girl, her father ran NBC. When he left there and tried to start a fourth network, he received death threats and subsequently lost everything. Weaver says,

✦ *...From my father, I learned that business was not fair. I knew that things did not happen in any kind of logical, nice way. I didn't believe that people necessarily got what they deserved. Knowing that the business was unfair helped me.*
Scott Poudfit, *Back Stage West*

✦ *We'd all be a lot better off if actors knew what went on behind the agent's door. There's not much mystery about what happens between the agent and the casting director, and the director and the producer, as a lot of actors want to weave myths about. Most of the time, the actor is just not right for the part.*
Kenneth Kaplan/The Gersh Agency

✦ *Careers are like pyramids. You have to build a very solid base. It takes a long time to do it and then you work your way up. No single decision makes or breaks a career. I don't think actors are ever in a position where it's the fork in the road or the road not taken, where it's, "Okay, your career is now irrevocably on this course. Too bad, you could have had that."*

If an actor looks at another person's career and says, "I don't want that," he doesn't have to have it. People do what they want to do. It's like people who are on soaps for twenty years. Well, it's a pretty darn good job, pays you a lot of money and if you're really happy, great. But if you're an actor who doesn't want to do that, you won't. Nobody makes you sign a contract. Again. And again. And again.

Every decision you make is a risk because it's all collaborative and it can all stink. Every play at the Public is not a good play. Not every television series is a piece of junk. People make decisions based on what price they want to pay, because there is a price.

If you don't want to work in television, there's a price. If you want to work in television, there's a price. If you want to work in New York in theater, there's a price. You have to decide if that's worth it; it's an individual decision, not a moral choice. It shouldn't be something you have to justify to anybody but yourself.

It's not about proving to your friends that you're an artist. It's about what's important to you at that moment. People can do two years on a soap and that can give them enough money to do five years of theater. And that's pretty important. It depends on why you're doing it and what you're looking to get out of it. What is the

big picture? Nobody knows it but you.
Tim Angle/Don Buchwald & Associates/Los Angeles

The second most favorite agent advice is about marketing and professional behavior.

✦ *I wish actors knew more about business things. It's hard. When people have gone through school for four years or eight years and have gone through wonderful*

~ ι ιιιιιⱄ υιι more about their union rules and regulations so that every time you get an actor a job you don't have to explain to them what the contract entails. That information is as readily available to them as it is to the agent. It's irritating to have to go through all that when you book somebody.
Jerry Kahn/Jerry Kahn, Inc.

✦ *Get a good picture that accurately represents you at your best. There are some photographers who take the most gorgeous pictures in the world and they don't look a damn thing like what the kids look like. You really want an accurate representation of who you are. It better be a look that you can duplicate when you walk into an office.*
Flo Rothacker/DGRW

✦ *Get seen. Do something to be seen. Visibility is the name of the game. You're competing for the attention of the casting people. You've got to do something to make them aware of your existence.*
Jerry Kahn/Jerry Kahn, Inc.

✦ *For the actor who wants to work all his life, the most important thing is continuity of management. Once you have established a reputation within the business that you are a good performer, the telephone generally rings. Your name is on a submission list. "Yes, she's right for this." "No, she's not right for that."*
Jerry Hogan/Henderson/Hogan

Being Smart

The world is small. The world of show business is even smaller. Be circumspect with your comments about other people's work, about auditions, about casting directors, and about agents. Los Angeles agent, Bonni Allen, underscores this truth.

◆ *Actors have to learn to keep their mouths shut except during auditions. Never talk in elevators. Never talk in rooms where you don't know people. Never. The bottom line is, "Don't talk."*
Bonni Allen/Bonni Allen/Los Angeles

Beverly Anderson is one of the most candid and entertaining agents around and she's been on the scene for a long time. When I asked her for her best advice, she thought for a moment and said:

◆ *Be smart. Don't be naive. If you're not smart, it doesn't make any difference how much talent you have or how beautiful you are. You're dead. In all my experience of thirty-nine years, of all the people that I can sit here and say, "They made it," they did not make it because they were the most talented or the most beautiful or even the best organized or the most driven. They made it because they were basically extremely smart human beings.*
It has nothing to do with the best looks and the best talents, the best voice or the best tap-dancing ability. It's being smart. Donna Mills is smart. Alan Alda is smart. Johnny Carson is smart. Barbara Walters is smart. They made it because they're smart, not because of talent. Talent is just automatic in this business.
Who's to say that Barbra Streisand has the best voice in the world? I mean, let's face it, she sings well and has gorgeous styling and she makes a great sound, but who's to say if she has the best voice? I think the one ingredient that counts the most in this business is "smarts". You could be talented and be sucked in by some agent who signs you up and never sends you out and you sit there for five years and say, "Well, I thought they were going to get me a job." Is that smart? To be smart is the best thing. Talent is a dime a dozen.
Beverly Anderson/Beverly Anderson

Part of being smart is factoring in what your dream may cost. An interview with *X-Files* star, David Duchovny, underscored a reality I have witnessed firsthand.

◆ *"I'm OK, I can take care of myself, but I feel isolated and lonely. I'm not happy. If I knew what it was going to be like, would I have taken the series? Can I also know what it would have been like if I didn't take the series?*

I hate those kinds of things, where people say, "Stop bitching, you could be working at Burger King now." As if those are the only two options for me, either act, or "Would you like a soda with your fries?" But doing a television show is like riding an elephant: it goes where it wants, with or without your say. Does that make me an ungrateful bastard?"

Martha Frankel, *Movieline*[10]

sign of negative thinking; how well you know which one you are. You will have just what you want.

Isn't that nice? It's all in your hands.

Wrap Up

Analyze

✓ how the business works
✓ who gets hired
✓ who hires and why
✓ which actor is getting your parts?
✓ what do they have that you don't have?
✓ your strengths
✓ your weaknesses

Important

✓ focus on the process not the goal
✓ study
✓ nourish your talent
✓ be organized
✓ acquire business skills
✓ be smart

6
Research & Follow-through

Unfortunately, agents do not send out resumes in search of clients. Even if they are looking for clients (and they are all looking for the client who will make them wealthy and powerful beyond their dreams), agents don't send out a list of their training, accomplishments and/or a personality profile.

Beyond their list of clients (which is not, by the way, posted on their door), there is no obvious key to their worth. Therefore, it is up to you to conduct an investigation of your possible business partners.

You have taken your first step. You bought this book. I have already done a lot of research for you by interviewing agents, asking about their background, looking at their client lists, interviewing some of their clients, and in general engaging in conversations with anyone and everyone in the business who might have something informed to say about theatrical agents. I've also read everything that I could get my hands on regarding agents and the way the business is conducted.

Agent Conversations

You should begin to have agent conversations with everyone in the business with whom you come in contact. If you are just beginning in the business and your contacts are limited to your peers, they will probably be just as uninformed as you. Never mind, ask anyway. You never know where information lurks.

Ask what they have done thus far to attract an agent. Ask if they have a list of agents they would like to have. Ask if they were able to get an agent to talk to them and why they picked that agent.

If you are in a group of actors and someone there is further along than you and has an agent, ask that actor for advice.

Tell him you don't want to be a pest, but that since you are just starting, you want to educate yourself toward an overview of agents and could he fill you in. Ask if he met with several agents first and what that was like, and if so, how he made his decision.

Find out how they approached the agent for the meeting, and how they knew to call that agent. It's okay to ask every dumb question you can think of, if you get permission from the person first and announce that you just want advice, not help, and that you are just there to learn. Try not to salivate. Don't totally monopolize the person. Ask your questions and move on, thanking the person for his or her time.

Take Your Time

Prepare yourself as an artist and as a business person so that you can operate on the level to which you aspire. If your work and presentation are careless, what kind of agent is going to want you?

+ *When an actor comes to meet me, I have researched him before the meeting and I expect that the actor will have researched me. When I see the actor has taken that time to do the research, that tells me that he also takes time to research the roles he wants to play.*
Flo Rothacker/DGRW

Get On With It/Agent Research

After you've digested this book completely, go back and read the agency listings again and take notes. You'll learn the agent's lineage, education, credits (clients), the size of their list, and have some idea of their style. If there is someone who interests you, check the index to see if the agent is quoted elsewhere in the book. Those quotations can give you additional clues as to how the agent conducts business, views the world, and how comfortable you might feel with him.

If you read his dossier and don't recognize any of the clients' names, that may just mean his clients are respected working actors whose names you don't happen to know, or they could be up-and-coming actors who have not yet worked. You can only evaluate the agent accurately if you know exactly what his list means. If he only works freelance, that tells you something too.

If the only clients the agent has on his list are stars and you are just beginning, that agent is too far along for you. If the agent has bright-looking actors with no important credits, he is building his list. If you fit that client category, perhaps you and the agent can build credibility together. It's worth a shot.

If you are an actor of stature, you will be looking for an agent that lists some of your peers. Some fine agencies have opened in the last two or three years whose names may not be as well-known as older agencies, but who have real credibility. Usually these are started by agents who interned at larger offices, learned the business, groomed some clients, and left the nest (frequently with some of the agency's choicest clients) to open their own agencies.

Once you have a list of agents who have caught your attention, if you are a member of any of the guilds, go there and peruse the agency/client listings.

Notice which agents represent the actors in your peer group. This will help you create your agent wish list. If you are not a member of any of the guilds, visit *Players Guide* and look through their book, raising your agent-consciousness by noticing the names and faces of clients of particular agents. Faces are frequently more revealing than names, but it's easier to get a focused picture of a particular agency looking at the SAG agency lists than looking at lots of pictures in *PG*.

SAG's agency listings (available only to members) give access to all agencies and their current client lists. A code identifies the size of the list and whether the clients are signed theatrically or commercially.

As your research continues, you'll have fantasies about the large conglomerate agencies. Check out Chapter Eight before you form your final opinion. There are many pros and cons to representation by star agencies at various levels of one's career.

While you are salivating about life at William Morris, consider that most stars come to celebrity agencies after a struggling independent agent helped the actor achieve enough stature and access of his own that the conglomerate agent felt his interest was financially justified.

William Morris, ICM and CAA do not offer career-building services. The large corporations are there to cash in on the profits. Although star representation enhances some careers, it is not true in all cases. In making your agent selections, make sure you are seeking an agent you have the credits to attract: Colin Farrell's agent is probably not going to be interested.

Make sure clients on the agent's list are your peers. It's all very well and good to think big, but you must walk before you run. Don't expect an agent who has spent years building his credibility to be interested in someone who just got off the bus. You must effectively agent yourself until you are at a point that a credible agent will give you a hearing.

I met a young actor with no real credentials who arrived in California and managed to hustle a meeting with an agent far above him in stature. The agent wanted to see a tape. Although he had l

agent, the actor totally lost all the hustle that undoubtedly appealed to the agent. Instead of learning from the experience and rethinking his approach, he did what many actors do. He blamed the agent.

When you're in pain, it's tempting to lash out at whoever is closest, but the common element in all our problems is ourselves. The day I figured that out, I was depressed until I figured out the plus side. If my problems were caused by others, I was powerless, but if the problem was me? Hey, I can change me.

✦ *I feel sorry for the people who spend all their time trying to use various forms of manipulation to get an agent while their contemporaries are working and learning. And the ones working at working will rise right up. The people who were assuming it's some kind of game will disappear.*
Fifi Oscard/Fifi Oscard Agency, Inc.

Who Do You Love?

At this point, you should have some idea of which agents appeal to you. Some names will keep coming up. Make a list. Even if you know you are only interested in Jack Menasche or Renee Glicker, target at least five names. You can't intelligently make a choice unless you have something to compare. You don't know that you like Agent A best unless you have seen Agent B and Agent C.

It's time to ask advice from casting directors with whom you have formed relationships. A CD who has hired you will probably be pleased that you asked his opinion. Tell him you are agent shopping and that you would like to run a few names by him. Also ask for any names he might like to add to your list. Listen to the casting director's opinion but, remember, he has a far different relationship with an agent than you will have. Make your own decision.

At this point your research is based on style, stature, access, size of list, word of mouth and fantasy. Let's forge ahead to face-to-face encounters.

Getting A Meeting

The best way to contact anyone is through a referral. If you know someone on the agent's list who will act as a go-between, this is good. If a casting director whose advice you have sought offers to call, this is better, but don't put the CD on the spot by asking her to recommend you. If you ask for advice about agents and she feels comfortable recommending you, she will. If she doesn't, be thankful for the advice.

If someone you contact just says, "Use my name," that is a polite brush-off. Unless a call is made, the referral is useless. Anyone can call and say, "Juliette Taylor told me to call." Unless Juliette picks up the phone, it doesn't count.

What Can Get You in the Door?

Winning an Oscar, a Tony, or an Emmy gets people on the phone. What else? If you are Young and Beautiful, just go drop your picture off in person (mid-week, late afternoon) looking as Y&B as possible. It is sad for the rest of us but true, that if you are really Y&B and can speak at all, few will require that you do much more. May as well cash in on it. If you are smart, you will study while cashing in since Y&B doesn't linger long and you may want to work in those gray years of your thirties and beyond.

You're not Y&B? Me neither. So this is what I suggest: If you are just starting in the business or don't have any strong credits, concentrate on classes. Join theater groups. Get involved with showcases. View as much theater, film and television as possible.

Notice names of directors and writers as well as actors. Begin making a list of the people you would like to work with. Align yourself with peers whose work you respect. Form a group that includes actors, writers and directors and focus on furthering each other's careers by working together.

If all you do is get together in someone's living room once a week and read the writer's new work or a current or classic play, you have accomplished a lot. Band together and buy a camera and write your own independent movie. You can buy a high resolution videocamera for $2500 that can actually shoot a whole film.

Check out the film school at NYU and see if you can leave a picture and resume. Read the bulletin board. Volunteer to do anything that needs doing and you will gain access to the Spielbergs of tomorrow. The Independent Feature Project (IFP) is also a good connection.

Don't approach agents and/or casting directors asking for meetings until you build up your resume and have something to show them. I spoke to an agent who told me that several young agent-shopping actors banded together and sent her a basket of goodies and among the goodies were their 8x10s and resumes.

This definitely got the agent's attention, the downside was that the actors were still just too green to be looking for an agent. Don't blow your chances by getting people to look at you before you are ready.

Once You Are Ready

If you have graduated from one of the league schools and/or have some decent credits and/or an Audition Tape (see Glossary), and have a clear idea how you should be marketed, it's time to begin. Send a letter to a specific agent, not the name of the agency in general, preceding the picture and resume by a couple of days. This is not a cover letter. A cover letter accompanies material. Single letters get read; pictures and resumes tend to sit on the "whenever I get to it" stack.

Make sure your letter is written on good stationery. The feel of expensive paper makes an unconscious impression that the writer is to be taken seriously. Say who you are and why you are writing. State that you are interested in representation, that you are impressed with the agent's client list (mention somebody's name) and that your credits compare favorably. If you have a particularly impressive credit, mention it.

I've provided an example below to stimulate your thinking.

Dear Mary Smith:

I've just moved to New York from Timbuktu and am interested in representation. I met George Brown and Sheila Jones in Jacqueline Segal's acting class. They told me they have worked through you.

Since I am in their peer group, I thought I might fit in with your client list. Although I am new to town, I do have a few credits. I met John Casting Director and have worked two jobs through him: *Hello Everyone* and *It Pays to Study.*

The parts were small, but it was repeat business and everyone has to start somewhere. I'm compiling an audition tape. My picture and resume will be in your office by Thursday. I'll call on Friday to see if you have a few minutes and might be interested in seeing my audition tape. I'm looking forward to meeting you.

Sincerely,

Hopeful Actor

A fabulous cover letter sample is on Andy Lawler's web page: www.geocities.com/Broadway/Mezzanine/4089/letter.html

I was told by an agent recently that the best way to get an agent to notice your picture is to walk it in. Don't attempt to chat up the receptionist, just deliver the picture in a manila envelope addressed to a specific agent with a note inside. He told me that hand-delivered pictures usually pique interest.

✦ *Most actors send their pictures out over the weekend and they all come in on Monday and Tuesday. If you sent yours on Wednesday and it arrived on a Friday, it might be the only one on the agent's desk.*
Peter Beilin/Peter Beilin Agency, Inc.

If you've just graduated from one of the league schools, mention this and some roles you have played. Make sure your picture and resume tell the truth and arrive when you promised them. If your letter has stirred interest, your picture will be opened immediately. Call the day after your picture arrives.

When you call (late afternoon is best), be dynamic and be brief. Be a person the agent wants to talk to. If he doesn't want a meeting, get over the disappointment and get on to the next agent on your list. Try to set up meetings with at least three agents and plan all the details of the meeting.

For starters, be on time and look terrific. This is a job interview

the agent asks, just say it wasn't working out. Agents are all members of the same fraternity. Unless this agent is stealing you from someone else, he will be at least a little anxious about why you are leaving. If you bad-mouth another agent, the agent wonders, subconsciously, at least, what you will say about him.

In general, don't talk too much. Give yourself a chance to get comfortable. Adjust to the environment. Notice the surroundings. Comment on them. Talk about the weather. Talk about the stock market, the basketball game or the last play you saw. That's a great topic. It gives you each a chance to check out the other's taste. Don't just agree with him. Say what you think. If you hated it, say it just didn't work for you.

This is a first date. You are both trying to figure out if you want another. If you've seen one of his clients in something and liked it, say so. Don't be afraid to ask questions. But use common sense.

+ *Be careful. It's not what you ask, it's how you ask it.*
Harry Packwood/Harry Packwood Talent

Phrase questions in a positive vein. Discuss casting directors that you know and have worked for. Ask which CDs the office has ties with. Tell the agent your plans. Mention the kind of roles that you feel you are ready for and that you feel you have the credits to support. Ask his opinion. Are you on the same wavelength? Don't just send out, make sure you are also receiving.

Find out how the office works. If you are being interviewed by the owner and there are other agents, ask the owner if he will be representing you personally. Many owners are not involved in agenting on a day-to-day basis.

Find out office policy about phone calls. Are you welcome to call? Does the agent want feedback after each audition? What's the protocol for dropping by? Will he consistently view your work? Will he consult with you before turning down work? Explore your feelings about these issues before the meeting.

If you need to speak to your agent on a regular basis, now's the time to say so. Does the office have a policy of regularly requesting audition material for their actors at least a day in advance of the audition? Let him know what you require to be at your best. If these conversations turn the agent off, better to find out now. This is the time to assess the chemistry between the two of you.

✦ *What makes a good agent? Partially the chemistry between an actor and the agent and partially the chemistry that goes on between the agent and the casting director; that they can communicate on an intelligent, non-whining wavelength. A good agent has to be able to not be so restricted by casting information and the Breakdown, so boxed in by what they read that they don't expand the possibilities. And finally, that they can get people appointments for good work.*
Marvin Starkman/Producer

During the meetings, be alert. There are intangible signs that reveal a person. Note how he treats his employees, if he really listens, his body language, how he is on the phone. How do you feel when he's speaking to you? What's the subtext?

The agent will want to know the CDs with whom you have relationships. Have this material available so that you can converse easily and intelligently. Even if your specialty is playing dumb blondes, your agent will feel more comfortable about making a commitment to a person who is going to be an informed business partner.

✦ *Morgan Fairchild came in, and out of the hundreds and hundreds of actresses and actors that I have seen and had appointments with, I've never been literally interviewed by an actress: "Okay, what have you done? Where are you going?" Incredible. She interviewed me. Yes, I was turned off to a degree, but I was so impressed by her brilliant mind and her smarts that I thought to myself, "Gal, even without me, you're going to go very far." She came in here and she knew where she*

Beverly points out an important truth. Although she was turned off by Fairchild's approach, she saw the potential. If you want an agent to want you, it's like any other relationship, you can't be desperate. It's important to be respectful, but don't genuflect.

a physical impression will be as strong as any other you can make. We want our new clients to be appropriate for the roles that are out there which are almost uniformly leading roles.

2. Unless you're another Kenneth Brannagh, avoid doing a Shakespeare scene. Such scenes are usually not as appropriate or as effective for an audience as contemporary material. And we assume that you can handle the classics, doing a scene raises the possibility that you may prove us wrong. On that note, avoid Moliere, Chekov and other classics like the PLAGUE. Outside the context of the plays these scenes come off as dull dull dull.

3. Shorter is better in regard to scenes. Most people make up their minds about you in the first twenty or thirty seconds. Don't drag it out. No scene should be longer than two or three minutes.

4. Funny is better than anything, if you can handle comedy. We sit through a lot of scenes, laughter makes us oh so grateful.

5. Try to avoid scenes that are done every year. The "Are You a Homo?" scene from *Angels in America* is so overdone. Aren't there other scenes in that play?

6. If you're going to do a scene from a film (which is fine) try to avoid

scenes with are linked inextricably to certain performances. Doing John Travolta or Samuel L. Jackson from *Pulp Fiction,* or Brando from *On the Waterfront* is bad. Why? Most of you aren't going to be able to compete with our memories of the original. Look at John Sayles' films, tons of great stuff in there.

7. Dress simply but to flatter. Guys should wear jeans or slacks and t-shirts or oxfords to show off their physique. Women should wear skirts or dresses and heels to do the same.

8. A showcase is NOT the time to explore your ethnic, racial, sexual or gender identity.

9. Don't do material just to shock or to tell us about the inner you. It more often than not, comes off as amateurish and polemic.

10. Finally, remember why you're there. It's not about art. It's about getting people to like you, to hire you, to sign you.

11. And a special tip from Jim Wilhelm (DGRW): Make us feel something. Good acting has the power to make us laugh or make us cry. In two or three minutes, those are the buttons to push.

Andy has even more information about preparing for your meeting on his web page at: www.geocities.com/Broadway/Mezzanine/4089

Closing the Meeting

Now that you have met the agent, given focus to him and his accomplishments, office and personnel, impressed him with your straightforwardness, drive, punctuality, resume, appearance, and grasp of the business and your place within it, it is time for you to close the meeting.

Make it clear that you are having such a good time you could stay all day, but you realize that he is busy and that you just have time to make your voice lesson. It doesn't matter where you are going. Just have a real appointment to go to and leave.

Suggest that you both think about the meeting for a day or two and set a definite time for when you will get back to him or vice-versa. If he asks if you are meeting other agents, be truthful.

If he's last on your list, mention that you need to go home and digest all the information. He will probably have to have a meeting with his staff before making a decision. Let him know you were pleased with the meeting. Even if it was not your finest moment or his, be gracious. After all, you both did your best.

My advice is to hurry home and write down all your feelings about

If the agent said he would get in touch with you and he doesn't, leave it. There are others on your list. If he forgot you, do you want him as your agent? If he is rejecting you, don't insist he do it to your face. Remember, you are choosing an agent. The traits you look for in a pal are not necessarily the qualities you desire in an agent.

If you want an agent on a higher level who's not interested, don't be deterred. There are other agents on that level. If they all turn you down, then perhaps you are not as far along as you think.

Don't be depressed. This just means you need to do more work on yourself until you are ready for those agents. If you feel you really must have representation at this time, you may need to pursue an agent on a lower level, but let's think positive.

✦ *There are clients I don't want to work with, not because they are not talented, but because I don't want to be in a constant relationship with them. They're not bad or good. They may be wonderful people, but it's not a good marriage. There is a better agent for them. You have to be able to feel you want to see it through the ups and downs. It's just personality. What's good for me might not be good for somebody else and vice-versa.*
Bruce Levy/Bruce Levy Agency

✦ *Some clients I would like to work with, but not sign. Someone who is sixty-five years old with that look is limited. Someone like that, I might want to represent on a freelance basis.*
Marvin Josephson/Gilla Roos, Ltd.

Good Manners

✦ *When you have a meeting with an agent, make sure you touch base with everyone afterward. Send a thank you note or a card and, if you do decide to go with that agent other than the one you were interviewing, just let them know how much you enjoyed meeting him and that you are appreciative of his time.*

Even if they say, "If you don't go with us, you don't need to call back," make the effort. If you treat people politely, you'll find that's the way people treat you.
Gary Krasny/The Krasny Office, Inc.

Making the Decision

Mike Nichols gave a speech to his actors one opening night:

✦ *Just go out there and have a good time. Don't let it worry you that the "New York Times" is out there, that every important media person in the world is watching you, that we've worked for days and weeks and months on this production, that the investors are going to lose their houses if it doesn't go well, that the writer will commit suicide and that it will be the end of your careers if you make one misstep. Just go out there and have a good time.*
Mike Nichols

I think that's the way many of us feel about choosing an agent. When I was in New York, I freelanced much longer than was career-appropriate because I was afraid of making a wrong decision that could have irrevocable consequences on my career. Gene Parseghian, who left William Morris to manage client Bruce Willis, says:

✦ *I find that actors are sometimes overly cautious. They are sometimes guided by anxiety or fear and that leads one to say, "No, I'm going to wait," when there is nothing to lose by signing with a particular agent who is interested.*

If it doesn't work, the actor can always get out of it. It's only for a year. There is so much more that can be done when there is an effective responsible agent at work that sometimes it's an actor's insecurity that holds him back, and I think wrongly so.
Gene Parseghian/Parseghian Planco, LLC

Not all agents share his feelings. Many would rather not sign you if they feel you are not ready for a long-term commitment.

✦ *I've had actors I was freelancing with say to me, "I'm going with," for example,*

"Fifi Oscard. I'm going to try it out and, if it doesn't work, in six months I'll leave." That tells me right away that I would never sign that person.
Harry Packwood/Harry Packwood Talent

What these quotations illustrate (regardless of the agent's point of view) is that the actor is questioning his own judgment. If you don't get in a position where you trust yourself and your instincts, how can you expect someone to hire you? How can you expect someone to put all

✓ peruse this book
✓ check SAG Agent/Client Lists
✓ study the *Academy Players Directory* and *Players Guide*
✓ consult casting directors
✓ don't underestimate word of mouth
✓ have face-to-face meetings

Tools to Set Up Meetings

✓ referrals
✓ good credits
✓ awards
✓ beauty
✓ audition tapes
✓ a well-written note stating your credits
✓ picture and credible resume

The Meeting

✓ be punctual
✓ act intelligently
✓ be well-dressed
✓ be focused
✓ know what you want
✓ ask for what you want

After the Meeting

✓ end the meeting
✓ set definite time for follow-up
✓ send a nice note

⚐ 7 ⚐
Kinds of Representation

Assuming you have your life in a fairly balanced state, have an

In New York it is possible to have several different agents submitting you for projects. The beauty of the freelance arrangement is that since not everyone sees you in the same way, there are many brains deciding whether you are right for a project, so you might get in on more things. Might.

But, it also takes more time, as you'll need to continue courting all those agents making sure to see all of them regularly and remind them of your activities much as if you were represented by a conglomerate.

The other downside (and the one agents hate most) is that according to Screen Actors Guild rules, in order to submit a freelance actor's name for a project, the agent must clear the submission with the actor before his name can go on a submissions list. You've got to be at the other end of the phone when he calls to ask if he can submit you. So if you aren't home or you're in the shower, you could definitely miss out.

Of course, it's possible you may not even get the chance to make the decision to sign because your career may not lend itself to exclusive representation.

✦ *Some people are better off not signing, possibly because they're the kind of actor that agents will only submit from time to time. The agent may not feel that the actor is very marketable and won't want to really work hard for him.*
Jerry Kahn/Jerry Kahn, Inc.

It's perfectly fine to freelance until you and the agent get a chance to know one another, but if you are an established actor and the agent has a track record, both you and the agent will expect to have a signed agreement right away. If you are just beginning your career, target several agents and freelance with them until you get a feel for who you like.

Exclusive Representation

A signed relationship with the right theatrical agent is a worthy goal. Don't be so afraid of making the right choice that you make no choice. Being signed can make your life a lot easier.

✦ *New York is much more of a signed town than it used to be. If you are going to have a career, you really should settle on someone because freelance is not the way to go. You don't get pushed. You don't get submitted for that many things and there is no development done, let alone any marketing.*
Gary Krasny/The Krasny Office

✦ *When I was just starting out as an agent, I did freelance, but as my career has moved forward, I realize I can't be as effective freelancing. I need to put that energy into working for signed clients.*
Flo Rothacker/DGRW

The agent makes his choice based on his belief that you will work and help him pay his rent if he submits you for the right projects. Once you and an agent choose each other, it is easier to stay in touch and become a family. It behooves you to put a lot of energy into the relationship so that the agent does think of you. If you are signed and your agent doesn't think of you, there are no other agents down the line to fall back on.

If you are smart, you won't give up your own agenting efforts just because you are signed. You'll just focus them differently. Too many actors sign and sit back waiting for the agent to take over all the professional details of their lives. The more you can do to help your agent, the better off both of you will be. Laurie Walton was an actress who decided to agent at her agent's office before she retired to become a Mom. Her perspective is worth mentioning because she has been on both sides of the desk.

Theatrical vs. Commercial Representation

Resume expectations of commercial agents are quite different than those of theatrical agents. Although this book is focused on agents who

agents require your name on the dotted line on a commercial contract before they will submit you theatrically. If that is the deal someone offers you, be wary. If they have confidence in their ability to get you work in the theatrical venue, they will not require commercial participation.

Many actors who are successful in commercials find it difficult to cross over into theater, film, and television and sign joint agreements only to find that they are never submitted with the agency's theatrical clients.

Theatrical vs. Commercial Success

Frequently, commercial progress comes swiftly and the actor finds he hasn't had work opportunities that lead to the same credibility on the theatrical level as he has had in the commercial world. He doesn't realize the agent does not feel comfortable sending him on theatrical calls because of the disparity between his theatrical and commercial resume. Until the actor addresses this, signing across the board is not a good business decision. There are many reasons, not the least of which is the contractual commitment.

Paragraph 6/Gone?

Paragraph 6 of the Screen Actors Guild Agency Regulations allows either the actor or the agent to terminate the contract if the actor has not worked for more than ninety-one days by sending a letter of termination. The actor can void his contract with an agent simply by sending a letter to the agent plus copies to all unions advising them of Paragraph 6.

As discussed on page eight, the defeat of the SAG/ATA referendum changed many things. The new General Services Agreement changes the terms of Paragraph 6 from ninety-one days to four months. As discussed on page eight, this is negotiable. Reread that discussion for more information on how to deal with this.

Whatever agreement you sign, the principle is this: If you have been working commercially, but are not sent out theatrically, you might want to find a new theatrical agent. However, since you have been making money in commercials, you cannot utilize Paragraph 6 to end your relationship.

On the other hand, if you have a successful theatrical career and no commercial representation and your theatrical agent has commercial credibility and wants to sign you, why not allow him to make some realistic money by taking your commercial calls?

People win commercials because they are blessed with the commercial look of the moment. It's easy to get cocky when you are making big commercial money and conclude that you are further along in your career than you are.

What you really are is momentarily rich. Keep things in perspective. Thank God for the money and use it to take classes from the best teachers in town so that you can build theatrical credibility.

It's possible to cultivate some theatrical casting directors on your own. A few are accessible. When you have done a prestigious showcase or managed to accumulate film through your own efforts with casting directors, theatrical agents will be more interested. It's all a process.

Signing Contracts

Consider carefully the commitment you make when you sign a contract. If you aren't making any money at all, it's tempting to sign with anyone who shows an interest. After all, a commission of 10-15%

or more of "nothing" doesn't seem like a big risk, but pretty soon, your "stumbling around" time will be over and you will be making money.

That employment may be the result of an agent or manager working for you but it may all come from your efforts. At the point that you're making money, anyone with access is going to want a piece of it.

You may have heard about actors who got out of their contracts easily, but I also know actors who had to buy their way out with a large financial settlement.

✓ requires vigilant phone monitoring
✓ gives you a chance to get to know the agent
✓ no overall game plan

Exclusive

✓ gives you more focused representation
✓ puts all your eggs in one basket
✓ allows a closer relationship
✓ it's easy to get lazy
✓ can backfire

Theatrical vs. Commercial Representation

✓ more financial rewards for commercial success
✓ all representation at same agency can block Paragraph 6 protection
✓ takes different credits for theatrical credibility

⚜ 8 ⚜
Star/Conglomerate Agencies

I guess we've all heard the joke about the actor who killed four people, ran over a baby, bombed a building, ran across the street into William Morris and was never seen again. It's the quintessential actor story about the wisdom of being signed by a conglomerate agency.

It does seems like it would be nice to have the same agent as Brad Pitt and Renée Zellweger, but is that really a good choice for you?

The question is perplexing and research doesn't support a definitive answer. As in all other important decisions — who to marry, where to go to college, whether or not to have elective surgery, etc. — your decision must be based upon a combination of investigation and instinct.

Research leads to the conclusion that star agencies (William Morris, ICM, CAA, etc.) have more information and the best likelihood of getting you in for meetings, auditions, and ultimately jobs, if they want to.

A successful writer friend of mine was repped by one of the large conglomerates. She was making about $150,000 a year and an employer owed her money. She kept calling her agent asking him to pursue it.

The agent was becoming increasingly irritated with her calls. She finally left when the agent said, "I really wish you were more successful and made more money so I wouldn't have to keep having these conversations with you."

If $150,000 a year is not enough to get the attention of the big guys, there are a lot of agents who will take your calls and treat you respectfully for a lot less.

What Do Casting Directors Think About Star Agencies?

I asked one casting director, "Who do you call first and why?" He answered, "CAA, ICM, William Morris" and mentioned the name of a one-man office. The casting director said that although he can cast all the interesting parts from the conglomerates, he dare not skip this particular office because everyone on the list was special and capable of brilliance.

He explained that although many prestigious independent agents have hot new actors, the process is like shopping for a suit. If you want the best suit, you go to Bergdorf Goodman first. At Bloomingdale's, you can get a beautiful suit and expect to spend a comparable amount of money, but Bergdorf has cachet, the perception that it is the source for the new and the unusual.

Casting directors also tell me they prefer dealing with DGRW. Th

star agents and succumb to a certain amount of blackmail. "Take this one or you don't get that one," for example.

It makes sense to choose an agency with a powerful client list, information and stature. However, when I met a well-known actress at a party, she had other thoughts. The Los Angeles based actress works mostly in film, but had recently been doing more theater, an activity not prized by star agencies since relatively little money is involved.

She ended up leaving the agency. "It's too much trouble to keep up with all those agents. They won't all come and see your work. Who needs it?"

I asked if she would return to the conglomerate if she got hot and her answer was illuminating: "I was hot when I was at the smaller agency. My name was on everybody's list. I didn't need to have a big office behind me. The only way I'd ever go back to a big agency is with a very strong manager. That way, the manager could call and keep up with all those agents. So, no, I don't think it's necessarily a better business decision to be at a conglomerate."

It's true that the conglomerates have more power and information, but do those attributes compensate for lack of personal attention? The strength of the large agencies comes from having a list of powerful stars and those bankable stars get the attention of the buyers and the agents.

Power Structure

When you have Colin Farrel and Julia Roberts on your list, you have the attention of the buyers. The kicker is that if you are Colin or Julia, you don't need star agencies because you are the power. If you are not Colin or Julia, you are filler.

A big star was in the final stages of closing a deal on a big new movie, when a higher-priced star at the same agency decided he was interested in the project. The original plans were shelved and the bigger paycheck did the movie.

An independent agent might do the same thing, but the chances are less likely that he will be representing you and your closest competitor.

Packaging

A large agency representing writers, directors, producers and actors, has a script written by one of its writers with a great part for one of its stars or first-billed actors. It then selects one of its directors and/or producers and calls ABC (or whomever) and says, "Our star writer has just written a terrific script for our star actress and our star director is interested. Are you?" ABC says, "Yes," and a package is sold.

Television pilots, TV movies and theatrical films are merchandised in this way. This phenomenon is called packaging. Non-star actors frequently choose agencies with package potential because they feel they, too, will get jobs out of the arrangement.

When John Kimble was still at William Morris, he told me,

✦ *You maybe can package the first-billed actor, maybe the second actor, but at that point people at the studios and the networks want their creative input.*
John Kimble

No Commissions On Packaging

If your agency packages a project in which you are cast, your agent is not allowed to charge commission because he is already getting a fat packaging fee from the production company. For an actor, this can be a good deal since you won't have to pay commission, but it offers no incentive for your agent to place you in the package.

He cares much more about the packaging fee and doesn't care much who is cast in it. And if you are tied up in a job for which the agent is not collecting commission, he is unable to sell you for something on which he can make money.

There are many horror stories recounting star clients who were never told of an offer of employment because the agent was withholding the star's services in order to get a packaging fee for the project. If the producers wouldn't go for it, the actor or writer or director never knew there had been an offer.

To the big agencies, it's all about money. They have a big overhead. But actors sometimes have different needs. James Woods, interviewed by Stephen Rebello spoke of a harrowing two years at CAA:

✦ *If there was anybody meant to star in a Tarantino movie, it's me. Ten days after I went with Toni Howard and Ed Limato at ICM, they sent me up to meet Tarantino. The first words out of his mouth were, "Finally, I get to meet James Woods."*

I'm sitting there thinking, "I haven't worked on a decent movie in two years and he's saying this?" I said, "What do you mean?" and he said, "I wrote Mr. So-and-So in 'Reservoir Dogs' for you."

I don't want to say the exact role because the actor who played the role is really wonderful. I said, "Look, I've had a real bad year, so could you explain why you didn't offer it to me if you wrote it for me?" He said, "We made a cash offer five times."

Of course, it was for less money than my [former] agents would want me to work for, but that's not the point. I wanted to cry. I'd rather work for a third of my salary and make "Reservoir Dogs." But I didn't get to do "Reservoir Dogs," didn't get to know Quentin, so I didn't get to do "True Romance" or "Pulp Fiction."

All because somebody else decided money was more important. They were treating me like I was an idiot ... I made less money this year doing six movies than I made when I was at CAA doing two movies. And I couldn't be happier.
Stephen Rebello, *Movieline*[11]

So all conglomerates are not alike. If you are going to exist at this level, be sure to do your homework. Ask friends, stay aware of what is going on.

✦ *The problem is that they're too big and they can't possibly function as effectively for an individual client as any number of not huge agencies. I don't see it, even for a star. I don't see the personal attention. To me, negotiation is easy. You keep saying no until you get what you want.*
Kenneth Kaplan/The Gersh Agency

Kenneth told me that when he was still an independent agent in New York. Since then, he has moved to The Gersh Agency, a bi-coastal agency with an important list of actors, writers, directors and below-the-line personnel. What does he say now?

✦ *Yeah. I know I said some things about conglomerate agencies in your last book. But, I have to admit that being able to work from the script instead of the Breakdown, which is really somebody else's interpretation of what the script is, plus access to directors and producers, really does take a lot of frustration out of being an agent.*
Kenneth Kaplan/The Gersh Agency

There are many prestigious independent agencies that have had a shot at the big time and chose to go back to a more intimate way of doing business. One of my favorite agents has groomed several stars. When those actors became more successful and demanding, the agent grew tired of being awakened at midnight to endlessly discuss the next career move. It was disappointing when the actors went to William Morris or ICM, but the agent just didn't see himself as a babysitter.

When Gene Parseghian was still at William Morris, he confessed that there were days when he wished he still had a small office with three or four people and twenty clients, tops. Since that time, Gene has opened his own management office, Parseghian Planco LLD, and now has a much smaller client list headed by his ex-William Morris client, Bruce Willis.

Sandy Bresler, a successful, distinguished Los Angeles agent (whose list includes Jack Nicholson, Judd Hirsch and Randy Quaid) left William Morris and started his own office. When that got too big for him, he left and started his own smaller office again. Of course, he did take Nicholson, Hirsch, et al. with him. That helped.

Conglomerates are not equipped to handle actors who are not

making a lot of money. They are not interested in building careers. They take you while you're hot and they drop you when you're not.

A friend of mine was on a soap opera for ten years while her conglomerate agent collected his ten percent. When she was suddenly written out of the script, she went for an entire year without an audition before she acknowledged her new career status and left for an independent agency.

ICM or CAA, Manhattan's real conglomerates.

If they are able to move your career forward quickly, you'll be well served. The conglomerates have access to not only the biggest star actors but to the star writers and directors who are mostly at those agencies or at United Talent (UTA) or Endeavor in Los Angeles.

But, if/when your career hits a snag and you have some downtime, as we've discussed before, the conglomerates have a very high overhead and they don't have time to waste nurturing careers. They can move you forward if you have the momentum. Once that's lost, you'll have to stoke it up again on your own because that's not the business those agencies are in.

A director friend of mine declares that CAA was marvelous for him when he had new product in the pipeline but when he took too long to make up his mind for his next project, the agents lost interest. Once he had a project again, they were the best at promoting it and helping him make his project a reality.

For insights into the business in all areas, particularly into life at the star agencies, I heartily recommend Mark Litwak's book, *Reel Power*. Although all of us may dream of the validation we might feel as a CAA client, as James Woods said in the Rebello interview, sometimes that validation costs more than we might like to pay.

✦ *All CAA thinks about is the biggest salary you can get, period. My [former] agents were saying stuff like, "If you star in a movie with so-and-so, and it makes*

$100 million, then you can work with anybody." I said, "You know what? I beg to differ. I don't think that if you do a movie with Pauly Shore, with all due respect, Sydney Pollack is then going to hire you."

Stephen Rebello, *Movieline*[12]

Manhattan Stars

ICM, William Morris and the newly resident CAA continue to be the power agencies in New York.

Until recently, ICM was considered to be far ahead of William Morris which had gone through lean times in the past as top LA agents Toni Howard, Elaine Goldsmith and Risa Shapiro defected to ICM because women agents at William Morris were not promoted.

But in 1999, William Morris managed to lure ICM co-chief, Jim Wiatt, as their president and co-CEO. When that happened, many star agents were not far behind, trailing with them their impressive client lists.

Now that CAA has moved to New York and spirited away star William Morris theater agent George Lane, William Morris may not be the most coveted place for a theater actor. Julia Roberts chose CAA over ICM when her agent left to head Roberts' production company. The landscape continues to change but, basically, these huge corporations have their fingers in every pie around. If you are big enough to go to any one of them, you can't go wrong.

◆ *For decades, the Hollywood pecking order was clear. There was always one agency that was dominant, though the top dog shifted over the years: William Morris, MCA, CMA, then CAA.*

But in a "Variety" survey, dozens of top studio execs and producers say something strange has emerged in the agency biz: parity. Newish tenpercenteries are hitting their stride as once indomitable firms hit some speed bumps, creating a competitive, nearly equalized environment.

"Variety" asked a substantial sampling of studio execs and producers, who spoke under condition of anonymity, to rate the five major agencies in five categories. Of those answers, there were only four "C" grades and one "A"; nearly everyone scored in the "B" range.

That's good news for most of the agencies, but may be unsettling for those agents who thought that their company was head and shoulders above the competition.

In a tight race, CAA came out slightly ahead, followed by Endeavor, UTA, William Morris and then ICM. Overall, on a four-point scale, only one-half point

separated No. 1 and No. 5.
  Claudia Brodesser, *Variety*[13]

It's been said that CAA's best strength is that is has the best client list and the strongest management team while ICM's strength lies in its movie stars, directors and lucrative television packages. William Morris still holds the keys to television and music.

Collect data and then use your research and instincts so you can

Nicolosi and other independent agents also have star clients and the access that goes with big name clients.

When all is said and done, the swell offices, script libraries, limos, flowers, and packaging considered, you'll make your decision based on what is important to you.

My vote would be for the prestigious, tasteful mid-level agency, but then, no one has plied me yet with limos and flowers. Who knows what I would do?

Wrap Up

Conglomerates

✓ have more information
✓ command more power
✓ have access to more perks
✓ can package effectively
✓ give less personal attention
✓ advice is corporate
✓ lose interest when you are not in demand
✓ have big rent; need big revenue

Distinguished, Smaller Agencies

✓ offer more respect
✓ offer more personal attention
✓ have more empathy
✓ might encourage riskier choices
✓ allow freedom for career fluctuations
✓ don't plie you with limos, candy or flowers
✓ probably have less information
✓ probably have less access

⚜ 9 ⚜
What Everybody Wants

If you could sign with any agent in town, which one would you

♦ *I want to know either that they work and make a lot of money so I can support my office, or that the potential to make money is there. I am one of the people who goes for talent, so I do take people who are not big money-makers, because I am impressed by talent.*
Martin Gage/The Gage Group

Beverly Anderson told me an instructive story about her reaction to meeting a prospective client

♦ *Sigourney Weaver asked to come in and meet me when she was with a client of mine in Ingrid Bergman's show, "The Constant Wife." She's almost six feet tall. I'm very tall myself and when I saw her, I thought, "God, honey, you're going to have a tough time in this business because you're so huge."*

And she floated in and she did something no one had ever done. She had this big book with all her pictures from Bryn Mawr or Radcliffe of things she had done. She opened this book and she comes around and drapes herself over my shoulders from behind my chair and points to herself in these pictures. She was hovering over me and I thought, "No matter what happens with me, this woman is going to make it." There was determination and strength and self-confidence and positiveness.
Beverly Anderson/Beverly Anderson

Part of Weaver's strength comes from having a strong, successful father/role model, Pat Weaver, producer of *The Today Show* and another valuable asset, a top-drawer education.

✦ *Training is the most important thing. I get very annoyed with people. Someone is attractive, so people say, "You should be in television," and then the actor thinks that's just going to just happen.*
J. Michael Bloom/Meridian Artists/Los Angeles

One of New York's most insightful and successful agents, the late Michael Kingman, was articulate about what drew him to an actor:

✦ *His talent. To be moved. To laugh. Feelings. Somebody who has contagious emotions. I'm looking for actors with talent and health, mental health and the ability to say, "It's my career and I devote my life to this." It's an attitude, not a spoken thing. It's an attitude that says, "Today is not the last day of my life."*
Michael Kingman

Geez, if we had mental health, would we need to be actors?

✦ *I'm looking for an actor with the ability to get a job and pay me a commission. I'm looking for people who are gorgeous and don't stutter. I'm looking for people who already have credits so I can sell them.*
Beverly Anderson/Beverly Anderson Agency

✦ *We are always looking for young people age fifteen to twenty-five who are savvy about the biz and have poise and talent. Good looks are extremely important to our TV and film contacts, so we are forced to make that important too.*
Dianne Busch/Leading Artists, Inc.

✦ *Come from a background of good solid training. I'm always attracted to the kids from the league schools, from good theater training.*
Bill Timms/Peter Strain & Associates, Inc.

✦ *The people we work with best are actors who are committed to their craft and are willing to do regional theater as well as off-Broadway and Broadway as well as film and television. The focus should be on training and growing yourself.*
Experiencing life so you can bring that to a character and to a performance. The interview part of the audition is just as important as the audition. Who you are as a person, as well as who you are as an actor.
Jim Flynn/Jim Flynn, Inc.

✦ *I'm drawn to actors who I feel are talented and have a commitment to win. I'll go through anything with an actor as long as his commitment is to win.*
Bruce Levy/Bruce Levy Agency

✦ *It always boils down to the talent. If somebody has a talent even though it's someone who's a drunk, you know that there's still the wonderful performance to be gotten. On the other hand, you must ask, "Is it worth going through all that to wait for that wonderful performance?"*
Jeff Hunter/William Morris Agency

✦ *I look for preparedness, humor — about the process of looking for work — thick-skin (unfortunately).*

...re you ready to make a phone call to Jay Binder and ask him to see this client?" That puts things more in perspective. And actors don't understand that I don't make the sole decision.
Laurie Walton

✦ *I want clients to come to me prepared, to have a sense of who they are, the kind of career they're likely to have, good self-knowledge, good reality about themselves.*
Phil Adelman/The Gage Group

✦ *If they're older and have been in the business and don't have some career going, it's harder because they're now going to be up against people who have many more important credits.*
Robert Malcolm/The Artists Group East

✦ *Since I am my own boss, I can choose who I want to work with. When a client approaches and I get even an inkling that this is going to be a high-maintenance client, I don't choose him.*
Jim Flynn/Jim Flynn, Inc.

✦ *I like performers who see themselves clearly, who have clear ideas of who they are, what they can do and I like them to be responsive to comments, criticism and advice born of having done this since 1949. Period.*
Fifi Oscard/Fifi Oscard Agency, Inc.

✦ *A spark. Something that's unusual. Usually from a performance. But, they can cool my interest by their behavior at our interview. You not only have to have the*

talent, you have to apply it. You can tell sometimes by their responses that they don't yet have that capacity.
Jeff Hunter/William Morris

Notice what Jeff said. They don't *yet* have the ability, that doesn't mean you're not going to. It doesn't even mean the agent thinks you're not going to. You just don't have it *yet*. Remember process.

What to Look for in an Agent

✦ *Schools sometimes give students a laundry list of questions to ask agents that the actors ask without even knowing why they ask them. When I meet an actor, I want to have a conversation with him out of which questions come.*

I think actors should have an idea of what they want to hire because they are hiring the agent. If I were an actor, I'd want to know that the agent and I were on the same page about the kinds of projects he would be interested in submitting me for. I'd want to know the agent's perception of my ability.
Jim Wilhelm/DGRW

✦ *One of the chief factors that determines the value of an agent is the amount of information that he has available to him. It is impossible for a small agent to possess the amount of information that a large agency can. We track hundreds of projects weekly at all of the studios and networks.*

If a client walks in and asks about a project, I can haul out 400 pages of notes and say, "Oh yeah, it's at this studio and this is the producer and they're doing a rewrite right now and they're hoping to go with it on this date and talking to so and so about it. I have that information."
Gene Parseghian/Parseghian Planco, LLC

✦ *The art of communication is extremely important. You have to imagine that apart from your lover, family, boyfriend, this is the person you are going to speak to more often than your mother and you have to not be intimidated to pick up the phone and have a conversation. Is that agent someone I want to talk to?*
Jim Wilhelm/DGRW

Busy Work?

Be practical in your assessment of auditions. Actors sometime grade their agents by the number of auditions they generate, not the quality or appropriateness. If you're not being sent on projects that you are right for, all those auditions are just for show. Producer and former agent, Marvin Starkman, has a realistic perspective:

✦ *If the actor/agent relationship were based on getting auditions for everything, then the agent would have a right to say that you must get everything he sends you out on. If you don't get everything he sends you on, then you have a one-sided relationship.*
Marvin Starkman

Ouch!

*...the moment you saw Jersey playing Gwyneth Paltrow's roles.
I could have been potentially interested in this woman in the areas in which she could work. But it was a turnoff, because not only do I know that she's not going after the right things so she's not preparing correctly, but she's not going to be happy with the kinds of things I'm going to be able to do for her. So I wouldn't want to commit to that person.*
Phil Adelman/The Gage Group

✦ *What's essential is that the goals the actor sets for himself and what the agent wants for the actor be the same. Or at the very least, compatible, but probably the same. If an actor walks in and I think that actor can be a star next month and the actor doesn't, it ain't gonna happen.*

If the actor thinks he's gonna be a star next month and I don't, it ain't gonna happen. By that, I mean it's not gonna work between us. Even though a great deal of it may be unspoken, there has to be a shared perspective.
Gene Parseghian/Parseghian Planco LLC

Size

A key aspect to consider in overall agent effectiveness is size. When we speak of size in relation to agents, we are speaking of his client list, the number of actors the agent has committed to represent exclusively.

One person cannot effectively represent a hundred people. It's like going to the store and buying everything you see. You can't possibly use everything, you're just taking it out of circulation and there are some agents who may sign you just to protect their client who is in your category.

It may feed your ego to be signed ("I have an agent!"), but if you are not signed with a credible agent that you can trust, you may just be taking yourself out of the marketplace. There are some agents who do just that.

Better to wait until you have the credits to support getting a better agent than to sign with someone who can't represent you effectively. Many agents believe a good ratio is one agent to twenty to twenty-five clients. An agency with four agents can do well by a hundred or even a hundred and forty clients, but that really is the limit.

Look closely at any lists that are extravagantly over this size. It's easy to get lost on a large list. It's all very well to have stamina, discern talent, have a short list, and be a great salesman. I take that as a given, but there are two other attributes that separate the contenders from the also-rans.

Access and Stature

The dictionary defines the word "access" as "ability to approach" or "admittance." Since the conglomerate agencies have many stars on their lists, they have plenty of ability to approach. If the studios, networks and producers do not return their phone calls, they might find the agency retaliating by withholding their important stars.

Stature on the other hand is different entirely. Webster defines the word as "level of achievement." Thus, Phil Adelman and Richard Astor certainly have more stature than some beginning agent at William Morris, but because Adelman and Astor don't have an equal number of bankable stars, they might not have as much access. Get both stature and access if you can, but if you have to choose, go with access.

The central issue is, how do you choose the agent who will provide the opportunity for you to be gainfully employed in the business?

Wrap Up

The Ideal Client

✓ has talent
✓ possesses contagious emotions
✓ displays a singular personality

The Ideal Agent

✓ is aggressive
✓ has stature
✓ has access
✓ is enthusiastic
✓ shares the actor's career vision
✓ has optimum actor/agent ratio
✓ has integrity

⚐ 10 ⚐
Everybody's Responsibilities

Once you have made a decision, there are many things to do. If you are switching agents, it's only right to have a face-to-face meeting to say goodbye. Say you're sorry it didn't work out and follow-up afterwards with a nice handwritten note saying the same thing. Make it a point to speak to, and thank, all your agents, as well as anyone else in the office for their efforts. Then pick up your pictures, tapes, etc. and leave. If the parting is amicable, buy your agent a drink if that's appropriate. You might want to send flowers. Send the necessary letters to the unions.

Setting Up Shop

The next stop is your new partner's office to sign contracts and meet and fix in your mind all the auxiliary people who will be working for you. If there are too many to remember on a first meeting, make notes as soon as you leave the office as to who is who and where they sit. Until you become more familiar with them, you can consult the map before subsequent visits.

Leave a supply of pictures, resumes and videocassettes. Be sparing. Bringing supplies is always a good excuse for dropping by. Also leave a list for each agent's file of the casting directors, producers and directors with whom you have relationships.

Alphabetize them if you ever want them used. Also leave lists of your quotes (how much you were paid for your last jobs in theater, film, and television), plus information about billing. The more background you give your agent, the better he can represent you.

Now the real work begins. Remember the agent only gets 10% of the money. You can't really expect him to do 100% of the work. That may be why you are leaving your old agent. You felt he didn't work hard enough. Maybe your expectations were out of line. Maybe you were lazy. Maybe you didn't keep his enthusiasm high enough. Maybe he was a goof-off. Even if that was the case before, it really doesn't matter now. What matters now is how well you and your new agent are going to function together.

90%-10%

The concept of 90%-10% is fascinating. How many of us have resented our agents when we have been requested for a job and all the agent had to do was negotiate? In fact, if all our jobs were requests, would we just have a lawyer negotiate and do away with the agent altogether? Or is the support and feedback worth something?

depression when my children left home. I willed myself to be up, but it was a loss that I had to mourn.

During that time, I was not particularly attractive to casting directors or anybody else. Life's processes must be endured. We can change agents and mates and clothes sizes, but we can't alter reality. We must experience it. Those realities are reflected in our work and ultimately enrich us as performers.

◆ *If you're not working because you are in your mid-life crisis, divorce, whatever, you may not be able to readily fix it, but it's up to you to assume you have a problem and set out to fix it.*
Martin Gage/The Gage Group

We can hope that agents are going to initiate work for us and introduce us to the casting directors, producers, directors, etc. What they are really going to do over the span of a career is negotiate, initiate meetings, arrange appointments when we are requested and, hopefully, support us in dark moments and help us retain perspective in our bright ones. Notice I say moments. Neither state lasts as long as it seems.

Because we are getting 90% of the money, we have to give up being cranky when we have to do 90% of the work. I assume you are willing to do that if you only knew what that meant. Let's talk about that.

What the Actor Can Do

✦ *The actor's job is to give me something I can go sell: a showcase, a new picture, a wonderful credit with a tour de force role. He has to be president of his own company, to treat the agent as his employee, to motivate him, to help guide him and to find a way to communicate with him so they can work as a team.*
Nancy Curtis/Harden-Curtis Associates

✦ *Trust me to have your interests at heart. Check you messages frequently. Live your life but let me know before you buy a ticket out of town. Keep up with what's happening. Always be as prepared as possible for your auditions.*
Dianne Busch/Leading Artists, Inc.

✦ *See everything you can, film, television, theater. What's filming in New York? What's the style of it? See who they are hiring. If there is something in town that has a part for you, go see it. Sooner or later, they're going to need replacements.*
Bill Timms/Peter Strain & Associates, Inc.

✦ *Stay positive and make sure you look good, be part of the artistic community where information is passed around and don't alienate your fellow artists.*
Diana Doussant/HWA Talent Representatives

✦ *I like our clients to be pro-active and to stay in contact with the office. Let me know if you have a special relationship with a director who's casting his new production. Information is a powerful tool. Keep you resumes updated. Return calls promptly. Remember, this is a partnership: both actor and agent working in tandem to build a career.*
Jeanne Nicolosi/Nicolosi & Co., Inc.

✦ *Develop some "radar" about the room, what they're open to across the table; it changes room-to-room and even hour-to-hour in the same room. Also, figure out how to act for "tape."*
J Kane/HWA Talent Representatives

Being an actor is an extraordinarily difficult job. You must be working on your craft and on your person all the time, staying abreast of what's going on and keeping your instrument tuned.

✦ *The actor has to be clear about what he wants and what he says. If he says he doesn't want to go out of town, but then misses out on an important project because it was out of town and gets mad at his agent, the agent is going to say, "Well, you*

said you didn't want to go out of town." Once you put qualifiers on your career, you are not going to have as many auditions.
Ellie Goldberg/Kerin-Goldberg Associates

✦ *Keep active. Even a lousy Scene class will help you put less pressure on auditions.*
J Kane/HWA Talent Representatives

✦ *It's very important for actors to network. If they have occasion to meet someone,*

acting class or in a small theater group or getting together with friends and doing a few scenes or sitting in front of a mirror and practicing a monologue, if you don't act every day, you're not an actor.
Bernard Leibhaber/Bernard Leibhaber Agency

✦ *You have to do a lot of work on your own. You sit around in circles with actors and everyone is saying, "Well my agent didn't get me in on..." Now that I'm sitting in this chair, I can see that even the agent's best efforts sometimes go unnoticed.*

You need the combination of the actors doing their work and trying to get themselves in. I tell actors, "If you know the musical director or the company manager, go to them. You may get in that way easier than I can get you in." Getting an agent is not the be all, end all of the way to get work.
Laurie Walton

✦ *Keep your acting wheel greased by doing readings. This is very valuable. Everyone does them. You get to know a group of people.*
Charles Kerin/Kerin-Goldberg Associates

✦ *If I have to take time from my day to talk to you to see how your day is going, then I'm not on the phone doing what I am supposed to be doing. If you hear of a project, make a two-minute call, "I heard about this, is there anything in it for me?" That's the way to be a good partner.*
Ellie Goldberg/Kerin-Goldberg Associates

✦ *Actors need to figure out what they want, why they are here. They need to have realistic expectations, get in to class and into some kind of focus group or form a networking group from their class. They need to surround themselves with people they respect, people who might be better than they, who are where they want to be. You can learn from others' achievements. You need to figure out a way to stay in touch with your family to help you stay grounded.*

Jack Menasche/Carlson-Menasche

✦ *Make sure that we have enough pictures and up-to-date resumes without our having to call. If you are a musical comedy performer, be willing to go to an open call if we have discussed this is what you should do. It's important to keep working whether it's in a class or a workshop or a group; always keeping your instrument finely tuned.*

Networking is important, but don't expect that every time your friend gets an appointment that you will too, and just because you call or drop in all the time, that we are necessarily going to think of you more. You don't want to become a pest. It is a business, in spite of how casual it is.

Gary Krasny/The Krasny Office

Put yourself in the agent's position. Everyone in the world is trying to get his attention, his clients and those who want to be. What would be the best way to get your attention under the circumstances?

✦ *Actors need to understand that until 11:00 or 11:15 in the mornings, agents need to organize for the day, set up what Breakdowns they have to do, solve all the problems and handle the calls that came in at the end of the day before and they need to prepare calls that have to go out for the first part of the morning. This is organizational time for the agents.*

If the actor can just wait until 11:15 to call to find out about their next important piece of news, they would receive a more favorable response from the agent. Anytime after 11:15 and before 4:30 or 5:00.

Gary Krasny/The Krasny Office

✦ *Eighty percent of the scripts come from books and those books are yours to read. If you've read a book and you think the part of Joe Blow is right for you, I don't see why you don't go out and get hold of the people who have those rights and say, "Look, I read this book. I'm a fan of this writer."*

Peter Beilin/Peter Beilin Agency, Inc.

✦ *Give me information I don't know about.*

Richard Astor/Richard Astor

♦ *You need to know who you can call on for help whether it's a producer, director, casting director or other actors. No matter what work you take, make sure it's work you are proud of. There is no use doing bad work for free.*
Jack Menasche/Carlson-Menasche

♦ *Get seen. Do something to be seen because visibility is the name of the game. You're all competing for the attention of the casting director. You've got to do something to make them aware of your existence.*

✎ Return calls promptly.
✎ Make sure your agent never gets a busy signal; get call-waiting.
✎ Take a picture and resume to every audition.
✎ Pay attention to the common sense details of keeping lines of communication open.
✎ Trust your agent and follow his advice from picture and resume to what kinds of shows to audition for.
✎ Make sure your picture is in the current edition of *Players Guide.*
✎ Provide your agent with ample supplies of pictures and resumes without being reminded.
✎ Go by and pick up the script before the audition.
✎ Arrive well-prepared and on time at the audition (build in time for emergencies).
✎ Don't try to date the receptionist.

Networking

I know that networking is a dirty word to many of you. You say, "Oh, I'm not good at all that" or "I don't want to get a job just because I know someone," or "I'm here for art, not for commercialism" or some other elevated actor-jargon we all use from time to time to keep ourselves from testing our limits.

The most effective networking is done with your peers. You're not going to be able to pal around with Jerry Zaks or Christopher Durang. But, you can pal around with the next Jerry Zaks and the next Christopher Durang by becoming involved with playwriting groups.

If you make it your business to attend theater wherever it's happening, you will begin to notice who the writers and directors are who are starting their careers. Focus on those whose work appeals to you. Let them know you like their work. Give them your card and ask to be on their mailing list.

After you've seen their work a time or two, let them know that you are available if they need anything. Become involved in their projects. You will all develop together. It's hard to break in to what seems like the charmed circle because people would rather work with people they already know and trust, particularly when a great deal of money is at stake. Wouldn't you rather work with friends and proven talent?

It is difficult behaving naturally around those who are higher on the food chain than you, but if you are well-read and cultivate an eye and ear for what's good, you'll soon contribute to the conversation and move up the food chain toward your goals, one rung at a time.

Don't You Really Want to Work?

I'm a pretty quick study and, with concentration, I have the ability to memorize audition material and not hold the script for something as brief as a commercial. When I was a beginning actor, however, I would always hold the pages, because my background had taught me to be self-effacing, and it seemed to me that putting the sides down was too pushy. It would make them think I really wanted the job.

On the day I decided to stop holding the script and take responsibility for the fact that I really did want the part, I began booking jobs.

I looked up self-effacing in the dictionary: it means self-obliterating. Don't do it. Sir Laurence Olivier used to ask anyone working on a project whether there was anything in it for him. If Sir Laurence could admit he wanted a job, am I going to pretend I don't?

Although I'm business-oriented about my career, I never thought about the 90%-10% aspect of things until I began researching my first book. I did think, when I finally signed with an agent in New York after successfully freelancing for a long time, that my own agenting efforts were over.

From the perspective of time and research, I realize that because I was passive and didn't educate myself, I missed out on entering the system sooner in a more meaningful way.

Some actors become angry when they have to tell their agents how to negotiate. They feel the agent is not doing his job if he has to

it. You are getting the 90%. Not only is it your responsibility, it's a way for you to be in control of your destiny in a business where it is too easy to feel tossed about by the whims of the gods.

Agents' Expectations

Before I talk about the agents' responsibilities, let's hear what agents expect from actors:

✦ *One of the things I expect from actors is that they love what they do. They may not love the getting the work part, but they have to be doing the work.*
  Peter Beilin/Peter Beilin Agency, Inc.

✦ *If I sign an actor for a year, I expect consistent callbacks. I expect, at least, growth. I'm not going to look at somebody's track record and say, "You've been out on fifty things here and you haven't booked a job; I don't think there's anything we can do here." It's difficult. It's very competitive. If I've believed in someone from the beginning, and if I see progress, if I see growth, and if I see the potential is still there, then I'm encouraged.*
  Kenneth Kaplan/The Gersh Agency/Los Angeles

✦ *I expect that they'll prepare the audition material ahead of time, they'll show up punctually, that they won't be afraid to go out on a limb and take some risks with the material, that they will return my phone calls promptly.*
  Gary Epstein/Epstein-Wyckoff & Associates

✦ *I expect my client to be on time, to be prepared, to be pleasant and to do the best job he can. Once I get you in the door, you are on your own. I think actors should not be afraid to take control of the situation. If they want to start over, they should say so.*

If they want to read different sides, they should ask for it. If they want to read another character, they should go for it. If they feel they were ignored, they should say so and not complain and whine to the agent.

The actor is a grown-up and casting directors are not demi-gods. They are people even though they have total control. I don't mean the actor has to complain, but he should make it known that he wasn't comfortable.

Gary Krasny/The Krasny Office

✦ *A client will say, "Are you angry with me because I didn't do so and so?" No. I'm giving you choices and opportunities. You make the decision and I'll go along with it. If I think it's a self-destructive point, I'll tell you. We can talk about it, but it's ultimately your decision.*

Tim Angle/Don Buchwald & Associates/Los Angeles

The agent puts his reputation on the line by sending you in. And in every audition, you put your reputation on the line by the quality of your work.

✦ *My job is to get the appointment. Your job is to show up, sell yourself and do your thing.*

Martin Gage/The Gage Group

Agents' Responsibilities: What the Actor Has a Right to Expect

All we want an agent to do for us is get us meetings for projects we are right for. This seemingly simple request requires of agents all the things that actors need to do; be informed and be professional, network, stay visible and communicate.

As we maintain our credibility by giving consistently good readings, the agent maintains his credibility. The agent has to build trust with the buyers so that when he calls and says, "See K Callan, you won't be sorry," the casting director knows he won't.

Then, if K Callan gets the job, the agent must be ready to do a wonderful job of negotiation, one that will make the actor (and the agent) happy and, at the same time, make the casting director feel he got a bargain.

The agent has all our responsibilities and more. The agent must maintain relationships with all of his clients and with the buyer. He must keep the buyers happy so that he can have return business.

Although no buyer hires you because he likes your agent, if your agent can't get you in, the buyer will never get a chance to see how talented you are. Once in the buyer's presence, it's up to you to make your agent and the casting director look good by your brilliant work.

- Call your agent at home other than in an emergency.
- Drop by the office unannounced expecting the agent to be available to talk to you.
- Expect your agent to deal with your personal problems.
- Arrive late (or very early) for meetings.
- Expect to use the agent's phone for personal calls.
- Hang around with the agent's staff when they should be working.
- Bad-mouth the agent to others in the business. If you have a gripe with the agent, take it up with him.
- Interview new agents while your agent thinks your relationship is swell.
- Call and say, "What's happening?"
- Expect the agent to put all the energy into the relationship.

Although many agents will be amenable to your dropping by, using the phone, and visiting with the secretary, etc., it's best not to take these things for granted. After all, you want these people to be free to do business for you. If they are talking *to* you, they're not talking *about* you.

If you are not feeling confident about yourself, go to class, talk to a friend, a shrink, whatever, but don't burden your agent with that information. Will he feel like using up his credibility by calling casting directors and telling them that you are the best actor since Meryl Streep, when he knows you can't even get out of bed?

If you are not up to auditioning well, tell your agent and postpone or cancel the audition. You are not only not going to be performing well enough to get the job, but people will also lose confidence in you and in your agent's instincts. It will be harder to get the buyer to see you next time.

Although the agent's main job is to get you appointments and negotiate, I believe you also have a right to expect him to consistently view your work and to consult with you before turning down offers. Your agent's advice regarding career moves is one of the things you are paying for. He is a conduit to and from the casting director and should convey feedback honestly about the impression you are making.

Make it clear you are ready to hear the bad with the good and you would prefer he express it in a constructive manner. Not "You did lousy," but "You were late," or "You were not prepared," or "The casting director said your energy was down." Let him know that you want to remedy any problems, but that you need to know what they are. It's hard to assess auditions accurately without feedback.

Some agents give advice about pictures, resumes, dress, etc., but, unless you are just starting in the business or have just come to the New York marketplace, established agents assume you have that all in tow. Your relationship will suffer if they constantly feel you are asking for their time in matters that are basically your responsibility.

That said, you may ask if your agent is interested in having input regarding pictures. This is the agent's sales tool (along with an audition tape) and he may feel strongly that pictures are one area where he wants to take time to advise you.

Sometimes I take my pictures to my agents for advice and sometimes I don't. My agents are busy and since they haven't made a point of asking me to consult them when I select new pictures, I frequently choose without their guidance. Sometimes, they don't think I made the best choice.

If I were writing a book I thought agents would read, I would suggest that periodically they call the actor in (whether the career is going well or not) and ask the actor to rate the agency. Is the actor feeling comfortable? Cared for? Serviced properly? An annual mutual rating wouldn't be a bad idea. Is the actor doing his part? Is feedback good? Pictures and/or resume need updating?

At contract renewal time, perhaps the agent himself (instead of an assistant) would call and say: "K, how are you? It's contract renewal time, I'd love to have you stop by and have a cup of coffee with me (lunch?) and have us talk about our relationship. We're still happy, we hope you are, but I'd like to get some input from you on what kind of job we're doing. Come in. We'll talk. We'll celebrate your contract renewal."

If I were suddenly a hot commodity, it would sure be a lot less d

J Kane/Peter Strain & Associates, Inc.

Staying In Touch

Keep in touch with your agent by being a good partner. Call with information that will give the agent something to do. "I just got beautiful new pictures," "I just did a mailing," or "I'm doing a show at EST." "Can I come in and have five minutes to talk about a mailing about how to reach people?," or "Hey, I just heard at my commercial audition about this series that's casting. The actress who is going in and I are always up for the same role, I know I'm right for it."

✦ *Give me a tool I can use. Actors need to do 50% and I will do the other 50%.*
Nancy Curtis/Harden-Curtis Associates

Los Angeles manager, Ric Beddingfield, says actors should make it a point to be seen by their agents once a week. Although most agents agree grudgingly that actors and their agents need to be in constant contact, most also agree that they hate the phone call that says, "What's going on?" They translate that into "Where's my appointment?"

It's like when you were little and your mom said, "What are you doing?" when she meant, "Is your homework done?" If you think about it from that perspective, perhaps you'll find a way to have a conversation that does not make the agent feel defensive. If you are calling to say you've just gotten a good part in a showcase, or just begun studying with a new teacher, or "Hey, did you see the new play at The Public? It's great, don't miss it," the agent is going to be a lot happier to hear your voice or see your face.

When Laurie Walton was still agenting, I asked how she liked agenting.

◆ *The only thing I'm not enjoying is that actors call me daily. It's tough. I would never be unkind because I've been there, but on the other hand, I think a lot of them are taking advantage and that's the part I'm not enjoying because actors can really be annoying.*

It's because everybody wants to work. I understand that hunger and need but it's interesting for me that they're not using their heads more and knowing that it's probably going to have the reverse effect.
Laurie Walton

A Los Angeles agent put it succinctly, "My worst day is when I talk to more clients than buyers."

The other side of that is that while you are taking the negative step of whining to your agent, you are avoiding taking some kind of positive action for your career.

Faxing

If you really really want to make a bad impression on an agent and guarantee that he will never be interested in you, fax him little notes, flyers and reminders of your existence. It may save you money and time to feed your flyer into his fax machine, but while you are doing that, you may well be disrupting his business.

If he is expecting a contract or a deal memo and his line is busy because he is receiving a flyer from you, it's not going to make him kindly disposed in your direction.

A non-obnoxious way to stay in touch presents itself when you drop off pictures and resumes. Call ahead and say that you are going to drop off new pictures and want to pop in, say hi or ask the receptionist if you can just stick your head in once you get there. Late afternoon is best.

You can just be in the neighborhood and drop by to show a new wardrobe or haircut. Then be sure to do that; just poke your head in. Don't sit down unless asked and if asked, stay no more than five minutes. Be adorable and leave.

If you are depressed and need to really talk, call ahead and see if your agent has time for you. Suggest a cup of coffee after work or, if he has time for a snack in the middle of the afternoon, you can bring goodies. Everyone is happy to see a treat in the late afternoon. Since many folks are on diets, bring something healthy.

Make the effort to speak to everyone in the office and call them by their names. Get to know your agents and their support staff on a person-to-person basis. Learn something about each one of them

~~~ ... ... you got a job and are going off to do something or whatever. Don't tell me, "Look I got this job; if you had sent me, you'd have gotten the commission." Tell me you had a couple of callbacks for something, or that you just got down to the wire on something, things that tell me about progress.*
Flo Rothacker/DGRW

✦ *We don't need phone-ins. We don't have the manpower. We encourage people to let us know when they are in showcases. Obviously, we can't go to all of them. We usually end up picking reliable ones. By that, I mean reliable by reputation of the theater, quality of production, the kind of cast they usually attract, and also the material. We stay away from showcases that do a lot of the classics. I don't think they're going to show the actor in anything we could sell them for.*
Peter Strain/Peter Strain & Associates/Los Angeles

It takes two energy-expending components to make any merger work. The agent must work hard for you all of the time and you need to deliver all of the time. If you don't stay abreast of what's in town, what shows are on television that might use your type, what you got paid for your last job, which casting directors you have met, who your fans are and/or if you are late or ill-prepared for appointments, the agent is going to get cranky.

If he doesn't drop you, he'll stop working for you. Worse, you'll get work anyway and he won't feel able to drop you. He'll just hate you.

If you are diligent and do everything you can do for your own career and consistently give your agent leads that he doesn't follow up on, then you're going to get cranky and leave.

It takes two.

Wrap Up

Details

✓ officially notify the previous agent that you are leaving
✓ take pictures, resumes, tapes, quotes, billing, etc., to new agent's office
✓ meet everyone in the office
✓ make map of where everyone sits

The Actor's 90%

✓ stay professionally informed
✓ network
✓ follow through
✓ communicate
✓ make informed suggestions
✓ get in a good acting class
✓ have call-waiting/dependable answering machine or pager
✓ check in and return calls promptly
✓ stay visible
✓ be loyal
✓ pick up the sides
✓ be punctual
✓ do great auditions
✓ give and get feedback

The Agents 10%

✓ arrange meetings with casting directors, producers and directors
✓ arrange auditions
✓ negotiate
✓ network
✓ maintain credibility
✓ communicate

◁ 11 ▷
Divorce

It's difficult to decide where to place information about relationships that don't work out. When I first started writing about agents, I began the book talking about this painful subject and vigilant folk pointed out that you have to have an agent before you can leave them. True, but some people who are reading this book already have an agent, and are contemplating leaving. They need guidance.

Don't skip this part just because you don't have an agent yet, you may learn some valuable lessons that will help you avoid a divorce in the future.

If an actor is not working, frequently he thinks it's the agent's fault and the actor fire him. The agent might not be the problem.

Valid Reasons for Leaving

If your agent won't return your calls, if he's been dishonest, or is not getting you out, those are legitimate reasons for leaving. Maybe you and your agent have different ideas regarding your potential. This is something that should have been ironed out before the contract was signed, but when that conversation comes later in the relationship, reality must be faced. Sometimes careers change and actors feel they can be better serviced by agents with a different set of contacts.

Perhaps your level of achievement in the business has risen. You have now, through brilliance or possibly a lucky break, become an actor of greater stature than your agent. This is very possible if fortune has just smiled on you.

Actor/agent relationships are just like any other relationship: as long as it's mutually rewarding, it thrives, when it's not, things must change.

Actors and agents seek each other for mutual gain. The agent must see money-making potential to be interested in taking on partial responsibility for your career. Thirty-five perfectly credible agents may pass on you and then agent number thirty-six will fall in love, send you to the right place with the right material and the right director, and you are suddenly a star.

It can happen the other way, too, of course. One minute you're hot and the next moment you're not. You didn't necessarily do anything so differently to get un-hot (frequently getting hot works the same way).

✦ *Jumping ship every six months (which a lot of actors do) only serves to hurt the actor because everybody knows about it and it shows that the actor can't necessarily get a job because something's wrong and it's not because of the agent.*
Gary Krasny/The Krasny Office

> one knows wnat to do with you.
>
> • You may be traveling into a new age category and have not yet finished the journey.
>
> • You might be getting stale and need to study.
>
> • You might be having personal problems that are reflected in your work; after all it's the life energy that fuels our talent and craft.
>
> • The business might have changed, beautiful people may be in (or out).

How many projects can you list that had parts for you for which you were not seen? And were there really parts for you? You have to be right for a part not only physically and temperament-wise, but you must usually have the credits to support being seen for significant parts.

✦ *Actors don't do their homework. What part would you have been sent up for on a Broadway show? Yes, it would have been nice if you, instead of Brad Pitt, played the part in that film, but no agent would have sent you up for the part.*
Bret Adams/Bret Adams

Maybe the reason you want to change agents is that your friend seems to be getting more auditions than you. It is hard to listen to others speak of their good fortune when you are home contemplating suicide, but before you get out the razor blade:

Consider

- Although you may frequently be seen for the same roles as your friend, there are aspects of your persona that are not the same.

- It cuts both ways. There have surely been roles that you were right for and your friend was not. You and your friend may be on different career levels.

- Perhaps your friend has not been totally candid in the descriptions of his auditions.

- It just might not be your turn right now. Be patient, it will be.

Measure your progress against your own development. Judge your relationship with your agent on whether or not it is mutually rewarding and respectful. If your agent has been dishonest with you or if there have been financial improprieties, those are valid reasons to leave.

Is Your Agent Doing His Part?

How can you tell if it's just not your turn, or if the agent isn't tending to your business? You can check with casting director friends, writers, directors, and anyone else you know in the business. If you are being as involved as you should be, you'll be abreast of current projects so that you will have a realistic idea concerning projects for someone like you.

Ask your agent what you can do to help get more auditions. Discuss casting directors you would like to meet. Have a list of two or three who cast material for which you are appropriate in both career and type.

Check with friends you trust to see if they have had any activity. Let them know you are not fishing for information, but just checking on your own paranoia. "Is my agent just not sending me out right now or is nothing going on?"

Drop by your agent's office with new pictures. Is the phone ringing? Are they calling other clients? Or is the place calm with inactivity? If the office isn't busy, this may give you and your agent a chance to chat.

Communication

.... .what it
.... s up to him to say, "Can I have a
... .. s veen too long?" And then we will say, "What have you seen that you weren't up for? Or what have you heard of?"

He might mention a project that he wasn't in on and we'll pull it out and see that on that project, they were looking for stars or younger or whatever. As soon as we talk about it, the problem is usually over. It's important, though, to have the conversation.
Ellie Goldberg/Kerin-Goldberg Associates

✦ *If the agent screws up a job, I think you should leave. If you don't get any appointments and you think you should be getting appointments, then you should move on to someone who is excited. If the agent doesn't take your phone calls, that's really a sign that there is something wrong. Sometimes you just have to get a fresh outlook. It works both ways.*
Gary Krasny/The Krasny Office

Bret Adams agrees.

✦ *I've heard actors say, "I haven't spoken to my agent in three months!" I've never heard an actor say, "I tried to get my agent on the phone for three months and I can't get through to him."*
Bret Adams/Bret Adams

If you are not getting auditions, that may make you unhappy enough to change, but make sure you are being realistic. If there are no parts in your category right now, a new agent can't change that. He might send you out on auditions you're not right for and make you feel busy, but you're still not going to get a job you are not right for.

Not everyone gets to do everything. Agents tell me the number one reason that a working actor leaves one prestigious, credible agent for another is that the actor sees his career in a different venue.

If he's on soaps, he wants to be on primetime. If he's a television star, he wants to do films. When an actor becomes a star in one area of the business, that means (among other things) that many people are constantly telling the actor how terrific he is and how he can do anything. That may not be true.

Research your peers. Have they made that change? Some people have enormous breaks come their way, but not everybody is going to make a movie and not every actor is going to do Broadway.

✦ *I think you know what you've been submitted for, how many appointments you've gotten. You have to take the explanation of the agent and weigh it.*
Jeff Hunter/William Morris Agency

✦ *Every agent has different contacts. I may have fabulous theater contacts and absolutely no film contacts. I might bullshit and tell the actor I have film contacts, but if you were that actor and I didn't get you a film audition for a year, you'd be getting the sense that what I was telling you is not true.*
Beverly Anderson/Beverly Anderson

✦ *We have to tell actors what we think they can realistically expect. That pierces their dreams sometimes and they move on.*
Jeff Hunter/William Morris Agency

The larger agencies are not in the business to handle less profitable jobs, so they either drop you or their lack of interest finally tells you that you're no longer on their level. This is the moment when you might be sorry you left that swell agent who worked so hard to get you started and engineered the big break for you.

Will he want to see you now? He might. He might not. It depends on how you handled it when you left.

Maybe your career is doing okay but you feel you haven't progressed in several years. Some actors leave their agents on a manager's advice. Sometimes that's a good idea, although it's possible the manager is just jealous of the relationship the actor has with his agent and the manager is seeking to put himself in a more powerful position.

Maybe you want to leave your agent because the magic has gone out of your marriage just as the magic can go out of a traditional marriage if both partners don't put energy into it. Check the discussion of the actor's responsibilities in Chapter Ten for ideas on how to infuse life into the partnership.

If you are both willing to save the alliance, that will · ·
energy and resourcefulness th·· ·
to kn··· ·

Just like anything else, if something is bothering you, speak up. Candor comes easily to very few people. Most actors have a need to be liked and it's not pleasant to confront people.

If you are not going out, call your agent and tell him you are concerned. He knows as well as you that you are not going out. Ask him if there is anything you can do. Ask if he has heard any negative feedback. Whatever you do, don't just start interviewing for a new agent and bad-mouthing your present agent.

It's easier to whine to bystanders about your dissatisfaction than to confront your agent, but that's not only a childish thing to do. It's ineffective, dishonest and makes you look bad. If you intend to succeed in this business, you'll have to do better than that.

◆ *Early on, at some moment, discuss problems with the agent. There are actors who hide in their kitchens, angry because they have not had auditions. By the time they can't stand it any longer, they call and tell you they're leaving. We're not omniscient; we don't know sometimes what is happening or not happening.*

We have meetings every week at the office and discuss all the clients and we might know someone is dissatisfied. But even if we miss it, you are obliged to come in and speak to your agent, not an assistant, because you are signed by the agent. Then we'll discuss it. We'll have a discussion and try to solve it.
Fifi Oscard/Fifi Oscard Agency, Inc.

Leaving Your Agent

If you did wait too long and it's too late for a talk, or if the talk didn't help, at least leave with a little class. Though it might be uncomfortable, get on with it.

+ *I would be very upset if someone with whom I've had a long relationship fired me by letter. I think it would be the ultimate rudeness, ingratitude, lack of appreciation for the work I've done. Get past the guilt, the embarrassment. I'm owed a certain consideration. Deal with it. I understand the difficulty, but that's not an excuse.*
Phil Adelman/The Gage Group

So be a grown-up. You owe your agent the courtesy of a personal meeting. Go in and talk to him. Explain that, for whatever reason, it's just not working. No need for long recriminations. No excuses. Not, "My wife thinks," or "My manager thinks." Simply say, "I've decided that I am going to make a change. I appreciate all the work you have done for me. I will miss seeing you but it just seems like the time to make a change. I hope we'll see each other again."

Write your own script, these words are just to spark your imagination. No need to be phony. If you don't appreciate what the guy has done and don't think he's done any work, just skip it.

Talk about the fact that you think the relationship is not, or is no longer, mutually rewarding. Leave your disappointment and anger at home. Be straightforward and honest and you'll both be left with some dignity. You may see this person again and with some distance between you, you might even remember why you signed with him in the first place. Don't close doors.

If you are leaving because your fortunes have risen, the meeting will be even more difficult because the agent will really be upset to see you and your money leave. Also, your newfound success has probably come from his efforts as well as yours. But if you are really hot and feel only William Morris, ICM, or another star agency can handle you, then, leave you must.

Tell him you wish it were another way but the vicissitudes of the business indicate that, at a certain career level, the conglomerates have more information, clout, and other stars to bargain with, and you want to go for it.

If you handle it well and if he is smart, he will leave the door open.

It has happened to him before and it will happen to him again. That doesn't make it hurt less, but this is business. He will probably just shake his head and tell his friends you have gone crazy and say, "This isn't the same Mary I always knew. Success has gone to her head."

He has to find some way to handle the rejection just as you would if he were firing you. It will not be easy to begin a new business relationship, but you are hot right now and the world is rosy.

Wrap Up

..... than Leaving Agent

✓ improve communications with your agent
✓ take a class, study with a coach
✓ do a showcase
✓ court casting directors
✓ put your own project together

Clear-Cut Reasons for Leaving

✓ lack of respect
✓ dishonesty
✓ communication didn't help
✓ differing goals
✓ personality differences
✓ sudden career change for better or worse

Speak to Agent

✓ before things get bad
✓ before interviewing new agents

⚞ 12 ⚟
Managers/TOS/Etc.

There are many avenues of thought as to the desirability of having a manager to help guide your career. Twice in my career (once in New York and once in Los Angeles), I had a manager. Not only did their service not enhance my career, but for the entire duration of each contract, I had no work at all. Since I had been working regularly before I took on the managers, you will find me a little biased against adding a manager to your budget.

Many feel that handing off their careers to a manager increases their cachet in the business. It may. It may not. Having a manager is really just having a second agent who is not regulated by the state or any of the unions, who may or may not have more contacts than your agent and may or may not be inclined to work for you, and is definitely going to cost you money if you book a job whether he had a hand in it or not.

If you seek a manager because you cannot get an agent, I'm wondering how you think the manager is going to help you. If the agent did not see anything marketable, is the manager going to create something? It could happen, but I'd want to see some proof that the manager is credible and not just latching onto every new face in town, hoping that somehow one of them will hit. In Los Angeles currently, there are 225 agencies and over 600 management companies. That ratio makes me suspicious.

Some excellent agents, hampered by outdated agreements with the performers unions and what they deem unfair/unregulated competition from managers, are choosing to dump their agency franchises and become managers themselves.

These people have credibility as far as I am concerned, but I wonder about all those people who just woke up one day and decided to call themselves managers.

I think a manager that is connected and in love with you could surely enhance your career. Although, as I mentioned, that didn't work for me though I had excellent managers who appeared to have both those qualities. You'll have to make up your own mind about this.

If you just graduated from one of the leagues and scored well in their showcases, many agents and managers may be giving you their cards. Don't let anyone rush you into signing anything. Check out all possibilities before you decide.

It's possible that a manager could get to you before you meet any agents and say, "Hey, don't bother meeting any agents, I'll take care of that for you when you are my client."

I see where they are coming from on that. If you are going to have a manager, one of the services you might expect w~~o~~uld ~~~ ~~~
your agent selection. H~~~~~ ~~
~ ~~~"

~~~~~ ~~anager, who is ~~~~~~~ about your career, can definitely make a difference, but so could the right agent.

When Julia Roberts came to New York (already connected because of brother, Eric Roberts) her manager, Bob McGowan, uncovered a part for her in the movie, *Satisfaction.* The part called for a musician, so McGowan enrolled Roberts in a crash drum course and enticed William Morris into repping her for the job.

So, if we had McGowan for a manager and happened to look like Julia Roberts and have her charisma, who knows what could happen?

And you know what did happen? Ultimately, Roberts dropped McGowan and opted for William Morris, and no manager, choosing to not have any more layers between herself and her employers. When her principal agent, Elaine Goldsmith, left William Morris to run Roberts' production company, Roberts moved to CAA.

Managers Can't Legally Procure Work

Although the law has rarely been enforced, managers are not legally allowed to procure work. That's the business of those people who have licenses from the state, you know, the agents.

◆ *LOS ANGELES, July 3 — Actress Jennifer Lopez has filed a petition with the California Labor Commissioner accusing her former manager of violating the state's Talent Agency Act by procuring employment on her behalf.*

The primary charge centers on whether Benny Medina was acting as her agent. Because Medina allegedly procured and negotiated work for her, the petition is requesting that all oral and engagement contracts she had with Handprint be voided. Those contracts saw her pay 10% of earnings from movies and television, 15% of her music, recording and publishing earnings, and 10% of her earnings from ancillary activities, including fashion and cosmetic interests.

Chris Gardner and Peter Kiefer, *Hollywood Reporter*,[14]

Actress Nia Vardalos is currently involved in a similar lawsuit against her former manager

✦ *The state court judge has refused to hear a challenge from Nia Vardalos' ex-manager to California's law barring managers from acting as talent agents. Tuesday's ruling by Los Angeles Superior Court Judith Chirlin sets the stage for the state labor commission to go ahead with a proceeding next week against Marathon Entertainment for performing as an unlicensed talent agent for Vardalos.*

The management company sued Vardalos in January for failing to pay 15% commission from her earnings from the hit comedy feature "My Big Fat Greek Wedding," which she wrote and starred in.

Dave McNary, *Daily Variety*,[15]

No one believes that Lopez and Vardalos have suddenly found religion and don't want to be in business with someone who is breaking the law. The lawsuits look like a way to avoid paying commissions and get out of a contract, but the fact remains that it's illegal for a manager to procure work for you.

And if he's not going to procure work for you, why would you be wanting a manager? There are other reasons, believe it or not.

When It Makes Sense to Have a Manager

Managers are a definite plus for child actors who need guidance and whose families have no show business background. A manager usually places the child with an agent, helps select pictures, wardrobe, monitors auditions, and some accompany the child to meetings and auditions.

If you are entering the business and need someone to help you with pictures, resumes, image, etc., managers can be helpful. There are, however, many agents who delight in starting new talent and consider this part of their service.

When you are at a conglomerate agency and it's too intimidating and time consuming to keep in touch with twenty agents, it might be advantageous to have a connected manager in your corner.

Changing agents is easier when you have a manager, because the manager does all the research, calling and rejecting of the former agent. If agent-changing is the only reason you have engaged the services of a manager, it's an expensive antidote to one uncomfortable meeting.

If you have the credits to support getting a good that on your own. If

ment, the actress went in , got the job, they called the agent to make the deal. The agent became more enthusiastic about the actress for a while, but ultimately dropped her. The agent's earlier disinterest signaled what he had already decided: that the actress was no longer appropriate for his list. In that case, the manager, though helpful, only delayed the inevitable.

Style/Substance

It's difficult to withstand a full court press from big time agents and/or managers, but remember, style is no substitute for substance.

I've never understood why an actor wouldn't want to have a personal relationship with his own agent. Unless you are an ogre with no interpersonal skills, I don't see the point.

On those two unsuccessful occasions when I did have a manager, the thing I liked least was that I was not supposed to talk to my agent myself.

A highly visible friend of mine recently lost a job because her manager discouraged her from speaking to her agent. The actress lost the job over money that would make no difference in her lifestyle. The agent might have prevailed in the negotiation.

The job was in a show that is now a huge hit and would have given real momentum to my friend's career. I kept saying, "Why don't you call your agent and ask what is happening?" Her reply? "I don't want to make my manager mad."

Come on! This is your career and you need to take responsibility for yourself. The more you hand off your power to someone else, the less control you have over your own destiny.

✦ *There are managers out there who wine and dine actors after the showcases and tell them not to meet with agents themselves and not to return their phone calls, particularly mid-level agents. Those actors might really be missing out. They should be meeting with the agents and making their own decisions. It's possible they don't even need a manager.*
Gary Krasny/The Krasny Office, Inc.

No License Required

There is no certifying group overseeing the activity or contracts of managers. Commission and terms of service are totally negotiable.

Don't be short-sighted. Have faith in yourself. Whether you are choosing an agent or a manager, don't just take the first person who shows some interest. Even though it may not seem that way right now, you have assets to protect: your face and your career.

You may say, well, so what if someone wants to charge me 25%. Right now, I am making nothing, if I make money, give this person 25%.

That's fine today while you aren't making any money, but when you do work, and you have a manager that is taking 25% and Uncle Sam taking up to 50% depending on your tax bracket, you will only be taking home 25% from all your work.

Tell Me Your Experience

I don't want to give managers a bad rap, so those of you who have or end up having managers, let me know how it goes, so we can all learn. My e-mail address is Kcallan@swedenpress.com. Note book title in reference line so I will know the mail is from a reader.

Top of Show/Major Role

A phrase heard more in Los Angeles than in New York, TOS/MR, refers to wages paid to guests in television episodes. Years ago, guest stars received $10,000 or more per week. In 1961, television reruns became subject to residual payments to actors. Production company managements got together and decided to stop negotiating with actors playing guest leads in episodes, setting a predetermined cap for appearances on half-hour and hour shows.

SAG minimum for principal work per day is $678 on a film or a television show, a very good fee. If you are fortunate enough to work for five consecutive days, however instead of 1

guaranteed number of days predicated on guest star billing. The fee difference between half-hour and hour shows is the guarantee; half-hour now guarantees five days employment at $678 per day, an hour show guarantees seven days. Days over the guarantee are paid at the same scale rate per day of $678.

There's nothing wrong in working for minimum if that is where your rate is, but management, by attaching the TOS/MR designation, throw the phrase around as though an actor is getting some kind of preferred rate. The real money goes to high visibility actors who routinely command $15,000 for an appearance on an hour show.

There are a few shows, notably those produced by Aaron Spelling in Los Angeles, that routinely break the top or have no top, but they also routinely hire stars whose fees are far above TOS/MR.

By and large, it has always been easier to negotiate for above-scale film and television money in Los Angeles than in New York. But even in Los Angeles, management has begun to cut supporting actors' wages in favor of the salaries of producers, writers and stars. Many esteemed character actors find producers stating, "This role pays scale plus 10%. Take it or leave it."

So sad.

The Breakdown Service

The Breakdown Service is a digest of all work available to actors on a given day and is available to agents and managers only. Before the Breakdown existed, agents in Los Angeles had to drive to every studio daily, read every script, make their submissions and repeat the process at the next studio.

Finally, an enterprising chap named Gary Marsh, who was doing just that for his agent mother, called the studios and said something like, "I think I could make your life better. If you give me all your scripts, I will summarize them and make a list of the types of actors needed for the parts, the size of each role, etc., and provide that information to all the agents. This will save you the nuisance of having all those people in your offices and them the inconvenience of driving."

Thus, the much-maligned Breakdown Service was born. It costs the agents a hefty amount, but it's worth it. When agents subscribe, they must agree not to show it to actors.

Some actors get their hands on the Breakdown, anyway. A woman in Beverly Hills charges actors $20 per month for access. She hides it under a rock behind a gate. Actors drive up, lift the rock, sit in their cars, read the Breakdown and make notes. They return it to its hiding place and drive away.

Whether or not it's a good idea to have access to the Breakdown is debatable. Casting directors already don't have enough time to look at all the agents' submissions. How will they ever be able to even open all the envelopes they could get from actors much less consider them.

◆ *It's just plain counterproductive for the most part [when actors get their hands on the Breakdown]. The casting directors are likely ignoring submissions from non-represented actors. And as far as represented actors go, you better hope you're wasting your agents' office time pointing out what you're right for. Our work is about everything after (and hopefully before) the Breakdown. We continue to talk to casting and find out so much. Often they want a name for a part, or are just looking for back-up ideas if their offer falls through, or change their mind about the "specs" after the first round of auditions, or cut the part, or a myriad of other factors.*

Casting is an activity and that means change, give-and-take, and yes mistakes happen. For an actor to pin his expectations to the snapshot in time of a Breakdown is wrong. Our office's response to an actor quoting Breakdowns is "that's not a mail-order catalogue there."
J Kane/HWA Talent Representatives

Whereas some actors are able to use the purloined information intelligently, others merely manage to alienate their agents. Though invaluable, the Breakdown doesn't include everything. Many roles aren't listed unless the casting director needs an unusual actor for a role.

Frequently, the script is truly not available. More times than not, the audition sheet will be filled by requests, not submissions.

Since not everything comes out in the Breakdown, it is important to assess your agent's other contacts. If your agent is not in a position to have more information than is in the Breakdown, that's still a lot of information if he uses it wisely.

g— — arrived in Marbella, I found myself standing next to the wife of the writer-producer-director at a party honoring the cast.

Making conversation and truly delighted to be involved with such a lovely script (Mel Frank eventually won an Oscar for it), I said to Ann Frank, "What a wonderful script. Is this Mel's first script?"

What did I know? I thought he was primarily a director and as, a New York actress, I was ignorant of things Hollywood. Ann was so cool. She neither walked away nor behaved in any way condescending. She just began patiently enumerating the edited version of her husband's incomparable credits.

It turned out that Mel was a famous Hollywood writer, and along with partner, Norman Panama, had written the Bing Crosby-Bob Hope *Road* pictures, plus many other classic films. I almost died of embarrassment, but Ann was all class. She patted my arm and smiled, "This will be our little secret." All the time I was apologizing for my ignorance, I was promising myself that I would never be in that position again.

If you have Internet access, it's a snap to power up www.IMDB.com, (Internet Movie Database) to check credits though I also recommend your library be stocked with books that tell you what the business is really like (*Adventures in the Screen Trade, The Season* and *Final Cut,* etc.), as well as biographies of successful people (in our business and others) that will provide role models in your quest for achievement.

Here is a list of books that will give your library a good start:

Aaron Spelling: a Primetime Life/Aaron Spelling
Act Right/Erin Gray & Mara Purl
Adventures in the Screen Trade/William Goldman
AFTRA Agency Regulations
A Passion for Acting/Allan Miller
Audition/Michael Shurtleff
Book on Acting/Stephen Book
casting by ... A directory of the Casting Society of America, its members and their credits/Breakdown Services
Comic Insights: The Art of Stand-up Comedy/Franklyn Ajaye
The Complete Directory to Primetime Network TV Shows/Tim Brooks & Earle Marsh
The Devil's Candy/Julie Salamon
Equity Agency Regulations
The Film Encyclopedia/Ephraim Katz
The Filmgoer's Companion/Leslie Halliwell
Final Cut/Steven Bach
Halliwell's Film Guide/Leslie Halliwell
Hollywood Agents & Managers Directory/Hollywood Creative Directory
Hollywood Creative Directory/Hollywood Creative Directory
How I Made 100 Films in Hollywood and Never Lost a Dime/Roger Corman
How to Sell Yourself as an Actor/K Callan
Hype & Glory/William Goldman
Indecent Exposure/David McClintock
The Last Great Ride/Brandon Tartikoff
The Los Angeles Agent Book/K Callan
Making Movies/Sydney Lumet
Monster/John Gregory Dunne & Joan Didion
My Lives/Roseanne
The New York Agent Book/K Callan
New York Times Directory of Film/Arno Press
New York Times Directory of Theater/Arno Press
Next: An Actor's Guide to Auditioning/Ellie Kanter & Paul Bens
Ovitz/Robert Slater
Rebel Without a Crew/Robert Rodriquez
Reel Power/Mark Litwak
Ross Reports Television & Film/Back Stage/Back Stage West Publication
Saturday Night Live/Doug Hall & Jeff Weingrad

Screen Actors Guild Agency Regulations
Screen World/John Willis
The Season/William Goldman
Theater World/John Willis
TV Movies/Leonard Maltin
Ultimate Film Festival Survival Guide/Chris Gore
You'll Never Eat Lunch in This Town Again/Julia Phillips
Wake Me When It's Funny/Garry Marshall

...keep my values in perspective. I need reminders of how easy it is to get caught up in the glamour, publicity, money, and power of this fairytale business. I need to remember that those things leave as quickly as they come.

I mustn't forget that success doesn't fix you. It may feel better for a while, but you're always you, just with a different set of problems. The more you read about people's journeys, the more perspective you gain.

For fun, read Tony Randall's book, *Which Reminds Me*. For inspiration, Carol Burnett's *One More Time*. To gain insight on how to get into and what goes on at film festivals, read Chris Gore's *The Ultimate Film Festival Guide*. Roseanne's book, *My Lives*, speaks candidly of the behind-the-scenes intrigue involved with her show. It's instructive.

Wrap Up

Managers

✓ can provide access
✓ can provide guidance
✓ take a larger percentage than agents
✓ are not governed by industry standard contracts
✓ minimum requirement: need to love you and be connected
✓ do your research

The Breakdown Service

✓ important tool for agents
✓ can be self-destructive in the hands of the wrong actor

Reference Library

✓ educational
✓ inspirational
✓ indispensable

⊲ 13 ⊳
Stand-Ups/Children

Abbott and Costello, Jack Benny, Chevy Chase, Jerry Seinfeld and
~~Ray Ro~~

▾ *we've definitely steered toward a very personality oriented comic. A charismatic style comic. "The Tonight Show" might use a comic because they're a very good comic in terms of their writing. A structural comic who writes a perfect setup and a punch line. Some of those comics wouldn't crossover into a sitcom because they might just be joke tellers. We want somebody who is a very full bodied character a la Roseanne, Tim Allen, Seinfeld. The development and casting people are looking for that. They are already walking in with a character. Some comics have stronger skills in that area.*
  Bruce Smith/Omnipop

In Franklyn Ajaye's terrific book of interviews with other comics, Jay Leno talked about his seven year rule.

✦ *"I've always told comedians that if you can do this for seven years, I mean physically make it to the stage for seven years, you'll always make a living. If you've been in the business longer than seven years and you're not successful, there's probably another reason. Sex, dope, alcohol, drugs - - you just couldn't physically get to the stage. Sam Kinison is sort of an example. He was funny, hilarious, but near the end he couldn't get to the stage anymore. No matter how popular you are, promoters are not going to rehire you if you miss gigs."*
  Franklyn Ajaye, *Comic Insights*[16]

✦ *A lot of comedy clubs across the country have closed, but there are still some in the Northeast so it's easier to keep a comic working there as they start to develop. The more stage time, they better they become. We encourage them to get into acting classes, not to become actors, but just to start. We want to know what their long*

range goals are. In order for a comic to become popular, he needs television exposure. If you can support that with a strong act, you're going to have a good career.
      Tom Ingegno/Omnipop

✦   *I wouldn't assume that just because you are a comedic actor that you can do stand-up. Soap opera people try to do stand-up. Most of them, because they are so pretty, have not lived that angst ridden life that comics have. It becomes a frivolous version of comedy. The first thing you want to establish with an actor that is going into comedy is: Do they have a natural feel for it? Do they have comedic rhythm for it? There are many actors who are wonderful with comedy, but can't do stand-up. You need the stage time.*
      Bruce Smith/Omnipop

✦   *A comedic person has to have the backing of theatrical training, otherwise you're looking at a personality-oriented project. Many stand-ups came out of theater and did stand-up as a means of survival.*
      Steve Tellez/CAA

✦   *I would say to really know whether you have any place in the comedy business at all, that you would have to give yourself at least two years. Less than that is not enough. The first year you'll spend just trying to get your name around, trying to get people to know who you are so they will give you some stage time.*

It's a long trip. Just like an actor. Don't seek representation with five minutes of material. You need to keep working. The next thing to do is to try to get work in road clubs. It's very important to get the experience. There is limited experience if you just stay in one city.
      Bruce Smith/Omnipop

The personal appearance agents that I spoke to supported what I learned from theatrical and literary agents. No one is interested in one shot representation.

If you get a guest shot on *Friends* and call an agent with that as an entree, he will probably take your call, but if you don't have a track record of credits (they don't all have to be as important as *Friends*) then the credible agent is not going to be interested. 10% of an episode is not enough of a payoff to put you on his list to share all his introductions and hard work.

If you have written a one-person show and Disney is interested, that might be interesting to a stand-up agent, but development deals go south with regularity and if you don't already have a stand-up career going for yourself, personal appearance agents are not going to be interested. They want people who have been playing clubs in and out of town and have the stage time.

Stand-up and performance artist shows are a bonafide way to be entrepreneurial about the business, but there are no short-cuts to theatrical/comedic maturity. You gotta do the time.

Children in the Business

...ably about the possibilities before you take the next steps. If your child is paying your rent, the balance of power tips and there is no more family hierarchy. Remember Macaulay Culkin.

That said, if you are still interested here's the procedure.

Professional experience is not necessary, but it helps. Children's agents don't expect professional pictures. Kids change too quickly, so it's a waste of money. Agents are perfectly happy to see snapshots of your child. Either mail them in with a note giving all the vital statistics: age, weight, height, coloring and anything the child might have done involving getting up in front of people and taking direction.

What your child absolutely must be is comfortable with people. Happy. Confident. Gregarious.

If the picture interests the agent, he will ask to see the child. He will want to speak to the child alone. Parents are invited out while the agent gets a feel for how the child handles the meeting that would be part of an audition.

If you are a child reading this, let me tell you that agents are very impressed when a child makes his or her own arrangements. It means you are motivated, organized and adult about the whole thing. A children's agent told me that her role model for a child actor was a client who at thirteen had done lots of local theater, called SAG, gotten a list of agents and sent in pictures himself. He got a manager and the manager got him the agent. He got the first job he went for: the national tour of *The Sound of Music*.

Children are paid the same per day as adults and will be (all things being equal) expected to behave as one. No sulking, tantrums or crankiness. They don't like it when adult actors do that either!

Set-Sitters

Parents should be prepared to ferry children to many auditions and, if the child books a job, to be on the set with him at all times. Not only is it a SAG rule that a parent or designated set-sitter of some type be provided, but it is never wise to leave your child in an adult environment on his own.

Someone needs to be there to be your child's advocate. No matter what the job or how good management is about things, they are in the business to make money. Someone must be there who is not afraid of losing his job if he speaks up that the set is too hot or the kid needs a break. We all want to please and do a good job, but certain rules must be followed.

You or your designated representative should be there. You should have both read the SAG, Equity and AFTRA rules so that you know when the child must be in school or resting or has a right to a break. You should also know about overtime and payment for fittings. SAG holds Young Performers Orientation Meetings on the third Tuesday of every month and is happy to provide guidance and support for its young members.

Many child actors work through managers. Managers can be helpful at this stage by putting a child together with an agent and making recommendations concerning dress, pictures, study and so on. Many parents fulfill the same role and many agents expect to provide the same service without an additional charge of 15%.

So saying, it's imperative that parents recognize their role in the process.

✦ *"What parents have to understand is, they are the excess baggage that comes along with the talent," says Innovative Artists' Claudia Black. "It's the parents' responsibility to make sure the child is prepared, on time and has rehearsed the scene."*

"....If agents can't get along with the parent, they won't take the kid. It's really not just about the kid being amazing," says Cunningham Escott Dipene's Alison Newman, "It's a joint thing, fifty-fifty."

Alexandra Lange, *New York Magazine*[17]

Wrap Up

Stand-ups

✓ need fifteen to twenty minutes of material to begin
✓ need a persona
✓ should have theatrical training

✓ are only half the package, it's the parents' job too

≈ 14 ≈
Researching the Agents

There are various categories of agencies: big, small, conglomerate, beginning, aggressive, just getting by. Since agency/client relationships are personal, any classifications I make is subjective. I'm presenting the facts as best I can, based upon my research and personal experience both in interviewing these agents and my years in the business. You'll have to take the information and make your own decisions.

There are new agencies with terrific agents building their lists who, like you, will be the stars of tomorrow. You could become a star with the right one-agent office and you could die on the vine at CAA.

There are no guarantees, no matter whom you choose. The most important office in town might sign you even without your union card if your reel and/or resume excites them, but mostly, they want you when you are further along. Whomever you choose, if you are to have a career of longevity, you can never surrender your own vigilance in the process of your career.

Evaluate Carefully

If you read carefully, you will be able to make a wise decision using client lists, the agents' own words, and the listing of each agency. It's unwise to write off anybody. In this business, you just don't know. One's own tastes and needs color the picture. I love my agent but you might hate him.

There are nice people who are good agents and there are nice people who are not. There are people who are not nice who are good agents and so on. Just because I may think some agent is a jerk doesn't mean he is. And even if he is, that might make him a good agent. Who knows?

If you read all the listings, you will have an overview. I've endeavored to present the facts plus whatever might have struck me about the agent: this one sold binoculars at the theater; that one was part of a sixties singing group.

Some agents have survived for years without ever really representing their clients. They wait for the phone to ring. Some agents talk a better game than they play. I believe it would be better to have no agent than to have one who is going to lie to you.

Agent Stereotypes

We all know the stereotypes about agents: They lie, that's their job. Well, some agents lie

...any who read this book are just starting out and will be scanning the listings for people who seem to be building their lists. Many of those agents have great potential. Some don't.

Who's Included in This Book?

I went through a real crisis about whom to include. Anybody who would talk to me? Only those agents that I could, actually in good conscience recommend? It seems inappropriate for me to try to play God about who is worthy and who is not.

On the other hand, I don't want my readers to think I would recommend everyone who is in the book. That automatically makes anyone not in the book suspect.

When I began writing these books, with the exception of the conglomerates, I only included agencies whose offices I could personally visit and interview. Today, in the interests of time and geography, there are a few that I have only met on the phone. The majority of the profiles are based on personal interviews.

Most of the time, I went to the office because that was most convenient for the agent and seeing the office refined my thinking about the agency. I didn't meet everyone in every agency or all the partners, but I did meet with a partner or an agent who was acting as a spokesman for the company. I could be wrong in my judgments, but at least they are not based on hearsay.

It's a good bet that if an agent is not included in the book, then I didn't know about them or had no access to information about them.

Number of Clients

The number of clients listed at the end of an agency profile only refers to actor clients unless otherwise specified and, just as the box office receipts reported in *Variety* might be inflated for business reasons, so too an agency may under report the size of the list. In reality, they may have more clients than they can reasonably represent and they would just as soon not publicize that fact.

The general agent-to-client ratio you should be looking for is at least one agent for every twenty to twenty-five clients. Anything over that, it's difficult to imagine a client getting much in the way of personal attention.

Screen Actors Guild Agency Lists

Most of the profiles in this book list a few clients from the agency's list, but some of the agents would not release any names lest they leave someone out. In those cases, they frequently give me a list and invite me to choose names. Sometimes I've gleaned names from trade ads paid for by the agency. Some information comes from trade columns devoted to information on artists and their reps.

If you are a member of SAG, you have access to any agency's client list. If you are not a member, you can consult the *Players Guide* leafing through the pages to see which agents handle which actors.

The material at *PG* is not as quickly accessible as going to the union and just pulling down an agency name and checking their clients. However, seeing client pictures pared with agent names might give you a more informed idea about a particular agency.

Take the time to do the research. It's worth it.

Less Is More

Once you feel you actually have something to interest an agent — an audition tape in your bag, a play in production and/or some swell reviews from decent venues — be discriminating in your quest for representation.

Don't blanket the town with letters. Target three agents that seem right for you and ration your money, time, and energy. It's more likely to pay off than the scattershot approach.

Agents are already inundated with reels and reviews, and while they are all looking for the next hot actor, there are only so many hours in a day. Don't waste their time or yours.

If you are just starting, don't expect CAA to come knocking at your door. Ch...

never buy another, if you see shoes that captivate you, you will buy them. The trick is to be captivating or, more specifically, marketable.

Body of Work

In my experience researching agents for actors, writers, and directors, I keep learning that agents are interested in a body of work. They want to see a progression of you and your product. They want to know that they are not squandering their hard won contacts on someone who doesn't have the ability to go the distance. They won't be able to buy a cottage in the south of France on their commissions from one job. Neither will you.

Like attracts like. You will ultimately get just what you want in an agent. I believe you can get a terrific agent if you make yourself a terrific client. There are no shortcuts. And today is not the last day of your life.

In her book, *My Lives*, Roseanne quotes a line from Sun Tzu's book, *The Art of War*, which she says everyone in Hollywood has read. It basically says: "The one who cares most, wins."

Kevin Bacon/Referrals

As you read the agency listings, you will see that many of the agents, though they will look at query letters, are not open to being contacted by new people who have no one to recommend them.

If you don't know anyone, remember "The Kevin Bacon Game" It's the same concept as the play/movie *Six Degrees of Separation* which contends that anyone in the world can find an association with anyone else in the world through six associations; in "The Kevin Bacon Game," it only takes three degrees and in some cases, less.

It goes like this. Your mother shops at the same grocery store as Kevin Bacon or, in my own case, I have worked with Tom Hanks who knows Kevin Bacon. Ostensibly, if I had a script I wanted to get to Kevin, I ought to be able to get it to him through Tom.

This all goes by way of saying that if you track all the odds and ends of your life, you should be able to produce somebody who knows somebody who knows somebody and come up with an authentic (however tenuous) connection to someone who can make a call for you so that you are not just querying/calling cold.

If you can't come up with a connection, you'll write the best darn letter in the world and knock some agent right on his butt. However, if you can score at "The Kevin Bacon Game" it would be best.

⚜ Remember ⚜

✓ Make yourself read all the listings before you make a decision.

✓ Mass mailings are usually a waste of money. There is no use sending William Morris or ICM a letter without entree. It's pointless to query someone you have never heard of. If you have no information about the agent, how do you know you want him? Take the long view. Look for an agent you would want to be with for years. Be selective.

✓ Don't blow your chances of being taken seriously by pursuing an agent before you are ready.

✓ Although rules were made to be broken, presuming on an agent's time by showing up at his office without an appointment or calling to speak to the agent as though you are an old friend, will ultimately backfire. Observe good manners and be sensitive to other people's space and time.

✓ Getting the right agent is not the answer to all your prayers, but it's a start!

15
Agency Listings

Agenc

roadway, #
at 51st Str
York,
2-5

at.

Whi
University
Glicker's tim
Because
other than
an intern
and fo
Yor

maili
provi
phone number,
computers goof, so call the office and verify
information.

They won't know it's you.

1406

et

NY 10019

81-1857

ctress for twenty years before she became
she knows where we are coming from.

double major in art and theater at the State
York, both departments competed for Renee
t lucky for her clients, her love of theater won out.
he'd been told that if you can be happy doing anything
eing an actor, you should (good advice!), Renee worked as
n audience development at a theater in Florida to test herself
nd that, yes, she really had to be an actress. She returned to New
k and scored a national tour of *They're Playing Our Song*.

Other national tours, cabaret work, commercials and lots of off-Broadway, television and films followed. Her day job (at night!) during that time was working as a waitress at The Comic Strip where she began to know all the rising young comics. Sitting on the sidelines watching the careers of Paul Rieser, Jerry Seinfield, and Chris Rock develop, she absorbed so much of the process that up-and-coming comics asked her to critique their work and club booker, Lucien Hold, asked her to help him open The Holding Company, a management business specializing in comics.

In 1995, when Renee heard that Abrams Artists was looking for someone to create a comedy department, Renee knew she was the one to do the job. Accompanied by her stable of comics, she joined the agency and took the place by storm, immediately booking theater, film and television sitcoms, sketch artists and improv actors.

When she decided it was time to open her own office in 1998, all but three clients came with her and those that didn't soon regretted their decision.

About Artists Agency is the first place casting directors call for comic actors of every stripe. Although Renee made her reputation with comics, she has impressive clients in film, television and theater, with a nice presence on Broadway.

The company's list of about fifty includes Ezra Knight (*Hack* and *The Lion King*), Laurie Kilmartin (*Tough Crowd with Colin Quinn*), Soara-Joye Ross (*Ragtime*), Kristine Zbornick (*Man of La Mancha, Bat Boy*), Craig Schulman (*Jekyll & Hyde, Les Miz*), William Ryall (*Amadeus, Some Like It Hot*), Eric Nieves (*Storytelling, NYPD Blue*), Dan Naturman (*Letterman, Conan O'Brien, Craig Kilbourn*), Tina Giorgi (*Craig Kilbourn*), Kevin Hagan (*Sopranos, Sweet Home Alabama, Third Watch*), Joey Vega (*Law & Order*), and Lou Martini, Jr. (*100 Centre Street*) Tricia Taff (*Little Shop of Horrors*) T

.... sure everyone knows that, she hosts a stand-up comedy showcase for the industry in January and August making sure her stand-up clients have been seen going into pilot season, as well as when the new season is up and running.

Renee says she never left acting, it's just that one day, she found herself in the middle of a new career and could hardly wait to get to work. She's really found her niche.

Renee has become the agent she wishes she had had when she was an actor. She's passionate about her clients' talent, supportive of their efforts and encourages them when they want to take chances.

Agents
Renee Glicker
Client List
50 plus

◿ Abrams Artists Agency ◺

275 7th Avenue
btwn 25th & 26th Streets
New York, NY 10001
646-486-4600

A brusk, efficient man, Harry Abrams has headed or partnered a string of agencies over the years: Abrams-Rubaloff, one of the commercial forces in Manhattan in the late 1960s and 1970s; Abrams Harris & Goldberg, a prestigious theatrical agency in Los Angeles during the early to mid-1980s; and currently Abrams Artists both in New York and Los Angeles.

Through resourcefulness, determination, an eye for talented agents and actors, Abrams has carved out an impressive bi-coastal agency that is respected in all areas of the business. He is quartered now in Los Angeles, running the motion picture and television department.

New York film/television head, Robert Atterman, began his career in the mailroom at ICM. The children's film and television division is run by Ellen Gilbert who worked her way through the training program at Abrams Artists.

Paul Reisman, Richard Fisher, and Jill McGrath join Atterman in the theatrical division, while Mark Turner heads a special department for hosting talent.

Clients come to this agency through referral, although they do look at all pictures and resumes.

Agents
Robert Atterman, Ellen Gilbert, Neal Altman, Richard Fisher, Jill McGrath, Paul Reisman, Billy Serow, J. J. Adler, Jonathan Saul, Alison Quartin, Amy Mazur, and Mark Turner.
Client List
95-100

⚔ Acme Talent & Literary ⚔

875 Sixth Avenue, #2108
enter from 31st Street
New York, NY 10001
212-328-0388

has embarked on a career in production and management.

The New York office is run by Nina Shreiber who decided while still an acting student at NYU/Tisch that a good way to find out about the business would be to work at an agency.

She worked as an intern for Mark Redanty and David Shaul at Bauman/Redanty/Shaul. She worked there as their intern and then assistant from 1995 until graduation in 1998, arranging all her classes on Thursday afternoon so she could be full-time at the agency. Although she wasn't there to persuade David and Mark to send her on auditions, once they actually sent her up for a job.

Upon graduation, saying that they could no longer let her work for almost-free, Mark and David offered her a real job. She told them she had to pursue her dreams of being an actress and they pointed her to two other fabulous agents, Bob Duva and Elin Flack, who were happy to have her come answer phones for them.

On her second day at D/F, her one audition (the European tour of *The Rocky Horror Show)* turned into a job, so Nina gave notice and set off to fulfill her dreams.

Although the tour was wonderful, Nina said it showed her that she really didn't want to be an actor. When she returned, she tried a job outside the business for a couple of months until Duva/Flack tracked her down and persuaded her to return to work for them.

From 2000-2002, she worked as their assistant and then junior agent and was so happy that when Lisa Lindo began wooing her to come to Acme, she didn't want to leave her home.

When Lisa finally made her an offer she couldn't refuse, heading the legit department at Acme, she made the move in May 2002.

The client list changed a bit with Nina's arrival. A few names from her list include Jeff Broadhurst (*Kiss Me Kate*), Renee Elise Goldsberry (*One Life to Live*), John Enos, Nick Gregory, Richard Kline, Erin Cottrell, Iris Almario, Liza Lapira, Tina Benko, Orlah Cassidy, Roberta Wallach, Celina Carvajal, William Blagrove, Ron Butler, Rick Hammerly, Joe Lo Truglio, Jimmy Palumbo, and Jayson Ward Williams.

Acme New York represents actors for legit and for commercials. Eileen Haves runs the successful commercial department.

The literary department of the agency repping writers, directors and emerging filmmakers is serviced by the Los Angeles office.

Agents
Nina Shreiber
Client list
50

⚒ Bret Adams ⚒

448 W 44th Street
btwn 9th & 10th Avenues
New York, NY 10036
212-765-5630

... movies and off-Broadway before he began a no-salary agent job in order to learn the business. He moved to Australia trying his hand at producing, creating an artistically successful, though financially shaky, theater.

From acting to producing to publicity and stage managing for Equity, Bret cut a varied path to his life today as one of the most reputable independent agents in New York at the agency he founded in 1971. In addition to all the other cool things he does, Bret is a crack backgamon player.

Margi Roundtree, Ken Melamed (Honey Sanders, Monty Silver), and Bruce Ostler are now Bret's partners at BA. Ostler is the primary agent for directors, screenwriters, and playwrights.

Actor clients include Don Stephenson (*The Producers*), Carly Jibson (*Hairspray*), Ron Holgate (*Urinetown*), Noel Harrison, Kenneth Haigh, Matthew Cowles (*Ed*), Valerie Perrine, and Charlayne Woodard (*Sunshine State, Unbreakable*).

This agency sees new clients mainly by referrals but they do check all pictures and resumes.

Agents
Bret Adams, Margi Roundtree and Ken Melamed
Client List
About 100

⚔ AFA/Agents for the Arts ⚖

203 W 23rd Street, 3rd floor
btwn 7th & 8th Avenues
New York, NY 10011
212-229-2562

Actress/singer/production stage-manager/director, Carole Russo, arrived in New York ready for work as a performer, but quickly realized she didn't have the emotional stamina for it. She chose the next best thing and uses her background to represent and nurture her list of clients.

Carole represented models at the Paul Wagner Agency and other modeling agencies before realizing that there were more creative ways to use her theater background. When she switched to the theatrical arena, her mentor was Fifi Oscard for whom she worked for five years.

AFA celebrated its twenty-fifth birthday this year, so clearly Carole learned her lessons well.

Colleague H. Shep Pamplin (H. Shep Pamplin, Oppenheim-Christie, Talent East) was an actor/director/producer/set designer before frustration at his inability to get agents and casting directors to attend showcases prompted his own agent, Bob Donaghey at Talent East, to suggest that he might be more effective if he just became an agent himself. So after a stint there, he opened his office in 1994, merging Oppenheim-Christie in mid 1997. He joined Carole in 2002.

Actors from Carole's list of about forty-five, are Michael Carroll, Paul Jackel, Ruth Miller, Jamie Chandler-Torns, Ann Van Cleave, George Riddle, Terri White, John D. McNally, Christian Whelan, Deborah Jean Templin, Sharon Alexander, Amanda Huddleston, Randy Aaron, Michael Phillip, Jeanne Montano, Berly Ellis, Peter Brown, David Lee, and Janet Aldrich.

Although Carole works primarily with her signed clients, she also works with some freelance actors.

Agents
Carole Russo and H. Shep Pamplin
Client List
45

✳︎ ⟫ Michael Amato Agency ⟪

1650 Broadway, #307
at 51st Street
New York, NY 10019
212-247-4456

... 1919, Michael moved to the other side of the desk opening his own office and carving a niche for himself representing some of the most important ethnic performers in the business.

Michael has a great eye for talent and spotted Marlon Wayans, Omar Epps, Esai Morales, and Lisa Videl, well before they became forces in the business. Billy Chang (*Law & Order: SVU; Martin & Orloff*) is one of the actors he freelances with.

Michael doesn't believe in signing talent and is always on the lookout for new young actors, so take heed: here is an agent who actively checks his mail.

Michael does a wonderful business in print and many of his serious actors pay their rent working in lucrative print ads, so if you have a real people kind of face, Michael might be interested in adding you to his extensive list of working print models.

Although Michael prefers referrals, he will look at actors with credible resumes and who have a VHS of their work. He will not look at tapes of theater work or film produced merely for audition purposes.

Michael is a great friend to animals and is active in many animal rights organizations.

Agents
Michael Amato
Client List
Extensive freelance and print clients

🐦 American International Talent Agency ✍

303 W 42nd Street #608
btwn 8th & 9th Avenues
New York, NY 10019
212-245-8888

Wanza and Claretta King have been in the business all their lives. Actors and singers, they were seeking a way to stay in the business when they hit upon the idea of starting their own theatrical agency. Since it's been thirty years, I guess it worked!

The Kings work with about thirty signed clients and a large list of freelance actors, comedians, dancers, choreographers, musical artists, young adults, teenagers, and children five years and older as well as variety and voiceover artists.

AITA also handles international companies of hit musicals requiring performers fluent in other languages. They book cruise ships so if you are interested in putting your club act together, AITA might be the agency to contact.

Some of their AITA's signed clients are Sandra Grant (*One Life to Live*), Phyllis Thornton and William Robinson.

Since this is an agency with a big freelance list, that means they really look at mail from newcomers.

This agency books for theater, film, television, commercials, voice overs, and special events.

Agents
Claretta King and Wanza King
Client List
30 plus freelance

◢ Beverly Anderson ◣

1501 Broadway, #2008
btwn 43rd & 44th Streets
New York, NY 10036
212-944-7773

the American Theater, *Sweet Bird of Youth*.

Beverly says that when she started agenting she was the youngest agent in the business. Now, she doesn't necessarily want to lay claim to being the oldest, but she does say she is the longest running agent and is still doing great.

In 2003, she had thirty clients on Broadway and on tours. Some of those clients include Jon Peterson (*Cabaret*), Sheila Gibbs (*The Lion King*), Angie Schworer (*Annie Get Your Gun*), Joy Lynn Matthews (*The Music Man*), Richard Pruitt (*42nd Street*), Frank Root (*42nd Street*), Mark Kaplan (*The Lion King*), Rusty Mowery (*Hairspray*), Daniel Herron (*The Producers*), Robert Ousley, and Kathryn Crosby.

Beverly constantly attends showcases always on the lookout for new young actors and she says that her greatest thrill is developing the careers of young artists. She works extensively with freelance talent but has a select list of signed clients.

Beverly Anderson is one of the key agents for the musical theater in Manhattan.

Agents
Beverly Anderson
Client List
15 plus freelance

'ent Agency, Inc. 📐

`reet, #711

'ue

'019

...Barbara Andreadis joined the family
...s. Like many of us, she left the business
...Her kids are grown now but instead of
...career, Barbara opted to continue mothering. Now
...or actors who, of course will always need her.
...trained at The Bonni Kidd Agency ultimately running that
...or two years before starting her own business in 1983.
...Andreadis says she "carries no generic types, only individuals." Her
...clients include Crystal Hunt (*Guiding Light*), Leif Riddell (*One Life To
Live, Oz*), Chance Kelly (*One Life to Live, Far From Heaven, Law & Order*),
Rosalind Brown (*Footloose, One Mo' Time, Law & Order*), Bertrand Buchin
(*As The World Turns*), Carolyn Ockert (*The Music Man, Annie Get Your
Gun*), Jacob Brent (*Cats*), Billy Hufsey (*Fame*), Greg Butler (*Chicago*),
Penny Ayn Maas (*Cabaret*), Karen Lynn Gorney (*Saturday Night Fever*),
Bernard Dotson (*Chicago*), Jill Nicklaus (*Movin' Out*), Lanene Charters
(*Mamma Mia*), Catherine Fries (*Beauty & the Beast*), Tony DeVito (*One
Life to Live*), William Mahoney (*One Life to Live*), Josh Adamson (*Taboo*),
Mark Manley (*The Boy from Oz*), David White (*The Full Monty*) and father
and son, Devin (*The Prince and the Freshman*) and Peter Ratray (*Law &
Order, Sex and the City*).

As you can see from the credits above, Barbara is one of the first
people casting directors check for good musical talent. She usually sees
people only by referral, but does look at all pictures and resumes.

Agents
Barbara Andreadis
Client List
50

↗ Irvin Arthur Associates ↖

1441 Third Ave. 12 C
New York, NY 10028
212-570-0051

existing clients.

Irvin says he is good about going to see newcomers the first time when they call and invite him, so make sure you are ready; he didn't say anything about the second time.

Agents
Irvin Arthur
Client List
20

 **Artists Group East**

1650 Broadway, #711
at 51st Street
New York, NY 10019
212-586-1452

In November of 1996, The Actor's Group (Pat House) and The Artists Group East (Robert Malcolm) merged offices. They could have called themselves The Actors/Artists Group, but decided to just adapt the name that Robert Malcolm adopted when he merged his New York agency (PGA, Inc.) with Los Angeles' existing Artists Group in 1993.

Robert commutes to the Manhattan office regularly but has handed over the reins to long time Artists Group East veteran and now partner, Cynthia Katz (Abrams Artists).

Robert and Cynthia are joined by colleague Daniel Grunes repping their list of 65 or so clients that includes Jerry Orbach (*Law & Order*), Michael Mulheren (*The Boy from Oz*), Tom Hewitt (*The Rocky Horror Show*), and Judy Kaye (*Mamma Mia*).

Artists Group East looks at all pictures and resumes.

Agents
Cynthia Katz, Daniel Grunes, Robert Malcolm
Client List
65

◿ Richard Astor ◺ *Keep in mind for showcases!*

250 W 57th Street, #2014
at Broadway
New York, NY 10107
212-581-1970

Richard was an actor in 1957, but a work-related back injury forced him to leave acting, so New York State's Workman's Compensation trained him for a new profession. Since Richard knew he wanted to be an agent, he chose typing and speedwriting.

He assisted agent Henry C. Brown and then worked for Lily Veidt and Harriet Kaplan before opening his own agency in 1960.

Retired teacher William Harkins came to Richard as an intern looking for a life in show business and definitely found it since he's now a franchised agent. He joins Richard in repping clients Vivian Reed, Anthony Chisholm, Chuck Patterson, Rex Robbins, and Carol Jean Lewis.

This office accepts resumes via referral only, but constantly tracks actors via showcases and workshops. If you do the work, he will find you. Freelance at this agency is only a first step toward signing and is a very limited practice.

Agents
Richard Astor and William Harkins
Client List
40

⊿ Atlas Talent ⊿

36 W 44th Street
just W of 5th Avenue
New York, NY 10036
212-730-4500

Atlas Talent is the only talent agency that I know of that bills itself as a broadcast agency. Not really a legit agency as Atlas specializes in actors for commercials both on camera and voice over as well as voices for clients like The History Channel and for promotionals across the board.

Pioneering the concept of ISDN (Integrated Switch Digital Network) whereby the voice can live in Los Angeles and work the New York job from his home over the telephone, has resulted in Atlas' impressive client list that not only boasts talent like New Yorker Bill Ratner (the voice of Channel 2 in New York and Channel 7 in Los Angeles) but also many celebrity voices like Eartha Kitt, Barry Bostwick, and Rip Torn as well as their strong list of anonymous celebrity voices that reside all over the country.

Atlas Talent was created in January 2000 by four senior agents who left Don Buchwald & Associates to set up their own shop: Lisa Marber-Rich, Jonn Wasser, John Hossenlopp, and Ian Lesser.

Before joining DBA, Lisa was an Account Manager in advertising at Bates, DMB&B and Foote Cone Belding, Ian Lesser was in film production at Tribeca Studio and Jonn Wasser was in marketing at Radio City and worked as a freelance entertainment writer with articles published in Detailsand other national magazines.

Michael Guy (Pauline's, Wilhemina) works with on-camera department head, Lynn Eriksen (SEM&M, DBA) while Melinda Zupaniotas (DBA) and Rachel Sackheim-Petrella (DBA) handle voice overs. Marilyn Macleir, who heads up Promos, was head of Creative Services at HBO, Lifetime and National Geographic.

Atlas also has an important Children's Programming department with puppeteer clients like Marty Robinson who built Audrey in *The Little Shop of Horrors*.

In addition to commercials and promotionals, Atlas' voice clients also narrate documentaries and long form narrations.

For more information about this agency, check out their website at www.atlastalent.com .

Agents

Lisa Marber-Rich, Jonn Wasser, John Hossenlopp, Ian Lesser, Lynn Eriksen, Rachel Sackheim-Petrella, Michael Guy, and Melinda Zupaniotas.

Client List

120 VO and on camera

✳ ⬿ Barry Haft Brown Artists Agency ⬾

165 W 46th Street, #2223
btwn 6th & 7th Avenues
New York, NY 10019
212-869-9310

Barry Haft Brown is one of the most productive agencies in town. Bob Barry maintained The Barry Agency for thirty-three years until late 1991, when Bob, whose discerning eye uncovered former clients Gene Hackman, Willem Dafoe, Christopher Walken, Scott Glenn, Maureen Stapleton, and Harvey Keitel, joined colleagues Steven Haft (Ambrosio/Mortimer), and Nanci Brown (The Gersh Agency) to form BHB.

Steve and Nanci have now moved on, but Bob continues to run the kind of agency that casting directors consult regularly and is now joined by John Camillieri, one of the rare agents in town whose background was totally in business.

Clients include Gordon MacDonald (*The Thin Red Line*), Louise Sorel (*One Life to Live*), Frederico Castelluccio (*The Sopranos*), Billy Lush (*Hack, Law & Order, State Side*), and John Spencer (*The West Wing*).

In addition to his acting career, client James Hanlon (*NYPD Blue*) is also a firefighter. He was in the process of shooting a film about rookie firefighters on 9/11 which became the Emmy and Peabody Award winning film *9/11*.

BHB's clients work in the theater, films, soaps, and in all areas of television. This agency only works with signed clients.

Agents
Bob Barry and Derren Capik
Client List
75-80

⚿ Bauman, Redanty & Shaul ⚿

250 W 57th Street, #2223
at Broadway
New York, NY 10107
212-757-0098

became partners. Mark handles things from New York and David helms
the Los Angeles office.

Redanty studied acting/directing at Ithaca College and got a job
working as a trainee for Raglyn-Shamsky Agency right out of college.
He became an agent while at R-S and then worked for Richard Astor
before joining (then) Bauman-Hiller in 1984.

Mark has been running the New York office since 1987 treating the
business and clients with the same care and class that the agency is
known for. This comfortable easy style is reflected in Mark's approach
to life and to the business.

He and colleagues Charles Bodner (Peter Strain) and Timothy
Marshall (who trained at RBA) preside over a list of not only
prestigious, but loyal clients.

Clients from their list include Victoria Clark (*The Titanic*), Mark
Kudisch (*The Wild Party, Thoroughly Modern Millie*), Donna McKechnie,
Glynnis O'Connor, Robert Morse (*Tru*), Sada Thompson, Scott Wise,
David Drake, James Earl Jones, Kristin Chenoweth (*The Music Man,
Wicked, You're a Good Man, Charlie Brown, Kristin*), Dennis Parlato (*Loving*),
Hunt Block (*As The World Turns*), Justin Deas (*The Guiding Light*), Ann
Guilbert (*The Nanny*), Liz Parkinson (*Movin' Out*), Dennis Christopher
(*Breaking Away*), Michael Nouri (*Victor/Victoria*), and Deirdre Lovejoy
(*The Wire*).

Clients come to this office by referral usually and work freelance
only as a prelude to signing.

Though Bauman died in 2003, Redanty and Shaul have elected to keep his name on the masthead maintaining that important historical link to the origins of this class agency.

Agents
Mark Redanty, Charles Bodner and Timothy Marshall
Client List
80

⩗ Peter Beilin Agency, Inc. ⩘

230 Park Avenue, #200
across from the Pan Am Builing
New York, NY 10169
212-949-9119

ᴜᴉᴍᴉᴜᴉꜱᴎ ᴉᴛꜱ ꞁoy ɪor nɪm, ᴘeter started oʈʈ workɪng as a page at ABC. He
quickly became the night program manager: the guy they leave in charge
when the important people go home. He produced for a while before
crossing paths with Noel Rubaloff who inspired him to become an
agent.

PBA looks for multi-talented performers. This agency's client roster
includes stand-up comedians, professional athletes, radio and television
personalities, singers, dancers, broadcasters, and sportscasters for both
television and commercials.

Agents
Peter Beilin
Client List
Freelance

⚔ The Bethel Agency ⚔

311 W 43rd Street
btwn 8th & 9th Avenues
New York NY 10036
212-664-0455

When the young Lewis Chambers was working in Admissions at Roosevelt Hospital, a doctor there thought Lewis would make a swell agent and introduced him to the owner of The Palmer Agency. Lewis joined her representing photojournalists from 1964-67.

He established his own agency in 1968 finding work for his photographers with such magazines as *Newsweek, Look, The Saturday Review*, and numerous foreign magazine publishers. A few weeks later, he entered the world of book publishers and added writers to his list of clients. In the 1980s, Lewis became franchised to represent actors as well.

Lewis now represents directors, actors, playwrights, novelists, and non-fiction writers. Details on his writing and directing clients are included in my books for writers and directors, but I must mention to you that he represents Michael Shurtleff's book, *Audition,* which I consider to be one of the best books about acting I have ever read.

Clients from his list include Marika Daciuk (*Mary*), Thomas Barbour (*Arthur, Girl Fight*), Mary Leight Stahl (*Phantom of the Opera*), Ivan Thomas, Marvin Chatinover (*Ed*), Susan Tabor, Mary Jasperson, Katharine Harber, Lucille DeCristofaro, T. J. Mannix, Loria Parker, Sandra M Bloom, Patrick Clayton (*42nd Street*), Maureen Griffin, Al. D. Rodriguez (*Pinero*), Wendy Coates, Hal Blankenship, Carlos Molina, Patrick Disney, and Mary Louise.

Agents
Lewis Chambers
Clients List
20 plus freelance

Big Duke 6 Artists, Inc.

6 W 14th Street, 3rd Floor
just W of 5th Avenue
New York, NY 10011
646-336-5080

...........g to have more control, Mike took Kelly and Julianna and, along with a French partner, started Despointes-Casey. When the agency moved to Paris, Mike decided to take a breather from the business.

It didn't take long for Mike to miss his calling. This time, in addition to having a cool agency, Mike fulfilled a fantasy by naming his business after Robert Duvall's helicopter in *Apocalypse Now.*

Big Duke 6 only represents clients for film, commercials and contract roles for soaps. He does not book day players and has no interest in theater or primetime television.

Three from his list of beautiful actress/models are Marissa Miller, Erin Cummings, and Larissa Drekonja, who Mike says is currently testing for "everything" and certain to be the "next big thing."

Agents
Mike Casey
Client List
19

⚖ Bloc ⚖

41 E 11ᵗʰ St, 11ᵗʰ floor
btwn University & 5th
New York, NY 10003
212-905-6236

Three childhood friends from Canada came south to create a dynamic new agency committed to representing the very best dancers and choreographers on both coasts and have quickly realized their goals.

Siblings Laney and Brendan Filuk's mother had a dance studio in Canada so it's no surprise that Laney is a dancer and that both Laney and Brendan are entrepreneurs.

Laney moved to Los Angeles to dance and act and ended up helping out her agent, Dorothy Day Otis with the dance clients. Brendan was working for SONY music when the Filuks hit upon a new idea, an agency with a focus solely on dance.

Although their friend, David Crombie had moved from Calgary to Seattle to work in technology, when Laney and Brendan suggested he join them in their Los Angeles adventure, Crombie quickly joined them. He spent a year learning the ropes of the new business before moving to Manhattan to open the New York branch of Bloc. Even though Bloc New York opened just a month after 9/11 in October 2001, the agency has prospered.

A case could be made that the name of the agency represents the names of its principals: **B**rendan, **L**aney, **C**rombie. However, the name was chosen for a more profound reason: bloc means people 'coming together for a common goal' which is just what these friends have done and is the focus of their agency.

The partners worked hard to create a Bloc 'brand' that represents the absolute best in dancers and choreographers. Producers and casting directors quickly responded.

You'll see Bloc dancers in all the Broadway Shows, on *Saturday Night Live, Carson Daly*, and scores of commercials as well as tours for Mariah Carey, Justin Timberlake, and others.

Their choreographers include Michael Rooney (Target, Kylie Minogue, eBay), Michelle Johnston (*American Dreams*), Laurie Ann Gibson (*Honey*), and Fatima (Gap, *Save the Last Dance*, Backstreet Boys).

A new addition to the client list is a top group of skateboarders to answer the growing advertiser's demand for this specialty.

David says Bloc looks for three things in clients: ability to dance, the look and a good attitude.

Agents
David Crombie
Clients
40

☒ Judy Boals, Inc. ☒
aka Berman Boals & Flynn

208 W 30th Street, #401
btwn 7th & 8th Avenues
New York, NY 10001
212-868-0924

Judy Boals started in the business as an actor, but a part-time job working with literary legend Lois Berman in varying capacities ultimately led not only to her agenting career but in 1995, to a partnership with Berman and talent/literary agent, Jim Flynn (Susan Smith, The New York Agency, Alliance Talent). Lois died in January of 2003.

In the spring of 2003, after seven years as partners, Judy and Jim mutually decided they wanted their own agencies and, since they were friends, decided to share space.

This is good news to potential clients who now just have to manage to get one agent to fall in love with them instead of two.

Both agencies continue to represent actors, directors, writers, and composers/songwriters who are chosen not only for their talent, but because they are easy to get along with.

Names from Judy's list include Charles Busch, Julee Cruise, Peggy Shaw, Dael Orlandersmith, Cheryl Freeman, Klea Blackhurst, David Mogentale, David Greenspan, and Ann Hampton Callaway. Clients come to this agency mainly through referrals.

There's good advice from Judy elsewhere in the book. Although Judy looks at all pictures and resumes, she rarely calls anyone in from them.

Agents
Judy Boals
Client List
50

⨳ Don Buchwald & Associates ⨲

10 E 44th Street
just E of 5th Avenue
New York, NY 10017
212-867-1070

Ricki Olshan heads the strong list of agents comprising the theatrical department: Rachel Sheedy, Allan Willig, and Joanne Nici. Victoria Kreiss, Missy Dweck, and Hannah Roth handle the Youth Division

There is also a Los Angeles office to help represent such prestigious clients as Louise Fletcher, Jay Thomas, Irene Bedard, Jay Sanders, and De Lane Matthews.

Agents
Don Buchwald, Ricki Olshan, Joanne Nici, Rachel Sheedy, Allan Willig, Missy Dweck, Hannah Roth, and Victoria Kreiss
Client List
100-150

⤳ Carry Company ⤶

49 W 46th Street, 4th floor
just W of 5th Avenue
New York, NY 10036
212-768-2793

Sharon Carry experienced and witnessed actor/agent and actor/casting director relationships as an actor. When she changed sides of the desk, she decided there must be a better way of interaction and vowed to make the business of acting a little less painful.

Her first priority as an agent was to make sure the actors were treated with respect. From the care exhibited toward clients when I was in their office, Sharon is definitely putting her plan into action.

Her agency represents ethnics, children, babies, athletes, stand-ups, actors and models. Carry Company was established in early 1991 with Sharon's agent training background coming from the modeling/print side of the business.

Sharon concentrates on their signed clients, but also works on a freelance basis. They have a pool of about fifty kids and fifty adults. Don't postcard this agency unless you have something real to say. "Hello, how are you?" doesn't count. They prefer flyers when you are doing something. Sharon says she takes flyers and work very seriously.

Agents
Sharon Carry
Client List
100

⊿ Carson-Adler Agency, Inc. ⊾

250 W 57th Street
at Broadway
New York, NY 10107
212-307-1882

...y ... colleague in the children's theatrical ...vision. In addition to her background in management at the National Black Theater, Shirley is also the mother of successful child actors, so, like Nancy, she intimately understands the challenges of her clients and their parents.

The successful commercial division is run by ex-child actor Bonnie Deroski, who thought she really wanted to leave the business, but finds that this is where her heart lies.

This office is clearly the place where casting directors shop for talented, trained, young legit actors. Their roster includes Alexander Goodwin (*Nobody's Fool, Mimic, Box of Moonlight, I'm Not Rappaport*), Bobby McAdams (*Minor Adjustments*), Steve Pasquale (*Miss Saigon*), Jessica Grove (*Miss Saigon, The Wizard of Oz*), Jessie Lee (*The Brady Bunch*), Tracy Walsh (*The Sound of Music*), Alison Folland (*All Over Me, To Die For, Before and After*), Donald Faison (*Clueless, Waiting to Exhale*), Frankie Galasso (*Jungle to Jungle, Hudson Street, Oliver*), Taryn Davis (*Snow White: A Tale of Terror*), and Lauren Pratt (*Object of My Affection, Second Day of Christmas*).

The agency has seventy-five signed clients for theater, film, and television. Carson-Adler looks at all pictures. They need not be professionally done to be considered.

Nancy has written the definitive "How To" book for young actors and their moms seeking work in the business, *Kid Biz*. It's available at most bookstores and libraries. It answers almost any question you might have about children in the business. I highly recommend it.

Agents
Nancy Carson and Shirley Faison
Client List
60

◢ The Carson Organization ◣

The Sardi's Building btwn Broadway & 8th Avenue
234 W 44th Street, #902
New York, NY 10036
212-221-1517

S.

...........ppportunities and nurturing environment
that has resulted in an amazing track record for clients Elisa Bocanegra (*Girl Fight, Resurrection Boulevard*), Lena Cardwell (*Passions*), Desiree Casado (*Sesame Street*), Latangela Missy Newsome (*Taina*), Chaz Shepherd (*7th Heaven, The Temptations*), Will Friedle (*Boy Meets World, Go Fish*), Tristin Mays (*Gullah Gullah Island, The Lion King*), Sharon Leal (*Boston Public, Legacy*), and Siri Howard (*The Sound of Music*).

This agency handles children and babies but not infants. Steve says they look at all pictures and resumes and have found some of the most important people on his list from the mail. They work freelance only occasionally and as a prelude to signing.

Agents
Steve Carson and Barry Kolker
Client List
80 plus very few freelance

✍ Classic Model & Talent Management ✍

213 W 35th Street 10th floor
New York, NY 10001
212-947-8080

225 W Washington, #2200
Chicago, IL 60606
312-419-7192

Though primarily a modeling agency, Classic is SAG franchised and says it represents actors of all ages, ethnicities, shapes, and sizes. In addition to all the jobs you might expect from a regular SAG franchised agent, they also provide talent for conventions, trade shows, industrials and print, so the avenues for paying the rent are expanded.

Classic talent can be seen in *The Haunted, War on China, Fate, Ambush, 1001 Lies, A Beautiful Mind, Sex and the City, Spin City, Law & Order,* and *The Sopranos.*

Classic has over twenty affiliate agencies nationwide and offers a wide range of talent including actors, print/trade show models, demonstrators, voiceover artists, celebrity impersonators, singers, dancers, foreign translators, magicians and more.

I didn't interview these agents personally so, I'm just providing information here. Web address: www.classicagency.com.

Agents
Mo Carpenter and Mary Depetris
Clients
Varied

⋙ CornerStone Talent Agency ⋘

37 W 20ᵗʰ Street, #1108
just W of 6ᵗʰ Avenue
New York, NY 10011
212-807-8344

.... Gersh and
.. ... office of his friend, legendary agent Robby
Lantz, Steve went along and Robby became his mentor and role model.

When Duva teamed up with Elin Flack (Duva-Flack), Steve made the move as an assistant, but moved quickly from assistant to sub-agent to being franchised in 1994. In September 1997, he created CornerStone Talent.

Colleague Mark Schlegel was planning to be a banker when he landed a job as a gofer for Mitch Leigh, working on *The King and I* as part of his studies as a communications major at Indiana's DePauw University.

That taste of showbiz torpedoed his banking career. Who could choose banking over show business?

His background somewhat mirrors Steve's since both began working for producers and worked with/for Robbie Lantz. Afterwards, Mark worked with Bruce Savan at APA and then returned to banking before Meg Mortimer and Louis Ambrosio (Ambrosio/Mortimer) lured him back into show business.

Mark left A/M joining J. Michael Bloom for ten years until Michael sold the business and Mark joined APA. A month after APA closed its NYC offices in February 2002, Mark joined Steve at CornerStone.

Their list of clients includes Angelica Torn (*Edge, The Sixth Sense*), Lee Wilkof and Amy Spanger (*Kiss Me Kate*), Jim Gaffigan (*Ellen, Welcome to New York*), Amelia Campbell (*Translations, Waiting in the Wings*), Lance Reddick (*The Wire, Oz*), Damian Young (*The War Next*

Door), Sean Martin Hingston (*The Long Christmas Ride Home, Contact*), Tsidii LeLoka (*The Lion King, Rose Red, The Diary of Ellen Rimbauer*), John Ellison Conlee (*The Full Monty*), Al Thompson (*A Walk to Remember, The Royal Tenenbaums*), Daniel Sunjata (*Take Me Out*), Marin Mazzie (*Kiss Me Kate, Passion, Man of La Mancha*), Peter Friedman (*Paycheck, Someone Like You*), Jayne Atkinson (*Enchanted April*), Lillias White (*The Life, Once on an Island*), Anna Belknap (*The Handler*), Sara Ramirez (*A Class Act, Capeman*), La Chanze (*Lucy, Ragtime*), Barbara Garrick (*Tales of the City, Sleepless in Seattle*), Anthony Arkin (*The Waverly Gallery, Power Plays*), Jamie Harris (*Fast Food, Fast Women*), and Robert Montano (*On the Town, The Yards*).

Shannon Kelly is Steve and Mark's associate. All three handle actors, comedians, ethnics, and seniors for film, soaps, theater and television. Clients come to CornerStone mostly by referral and at this point, their list is full unless they see another talented actor they absolutely cannot resist.

Agents
Steve Stone, Mark Schlegel, and Shannon Kelly
Client List
75

⤴ CAA/Creative Artists Agency ⤸

Youth Intelligence Offices
9 W 10th Street
just W of 5th Avenue
New York, NY 10011
212-982-5428

...owed Lane to Gotham's CAA office.

CAA was founded in 1975 by Michael Ovitz, Bill Haber, Rowland Perkins, Ron Meyer, and Michael Rosenfield.

✦ *When these dynamic men left William Morris to start the agency, they ...didn't have any clients. They didn't have any financing. They didn't have any offices. In fact, between the five of them, they only had one car...They couldn't afford to hire a receptionist. So each of their wives filled in one day a week.*
Charles Schreger, *Los Angeles Times*[18]

Though the founding fathers are gone, president Richard Lovett, co-chairs Lee Gabler and Rick Nicita, and senior vice-president Michael Rosenfeld have managed to keep the agency's status in tact, although William Morris, UTA and ICM are nipping ferociously at their heels.

Variety editor Peter Bart recently wrote a love letter to CAA.

✦ *This week... I reviewed the latest developments at CAA. Having vowed never to open a New York office, CAA hired an accomplished theatrical agent, George Lane, away from William Morris, proclaiming its intention to become a force on Broadway. At the same time, it signed a few other top players in music and TV and was enmeshed in a series of high-profile movie deals.*

It also acquired a market research company and was expanding its relationships with major advertisers who were eager to forge links with CAA's roster of celebrities.

Clients of the agency gladly volunteer their analyses of the CAA work ethic. You

feel the whole place is behind you, says one director who asked not to be quoted. You don't feel you're represented by a lone agent, while the guy in the next office is trying to get your job for someone else.
Peter Bart, *Variety*[19]

CAA guards client information carefully but in August 1999 the *Los Angeles Times* reported that CAA had 125 agents and about 1,200 clients.

That's about one agent for every nine clients. I doubt that time considerations break down that way, so if you're not Tom Hanks or Meryl Streep, you surely won't get as much attention as they, but still, having CAA say your name would be worth a lot.

Clients include the cream of theater, film and television talent: Julia Roberts, Hilary Swank, Gwyneth Paltrow, Helen Hunt, Renee Zellweger, Sandra Bullock, Cameron Diaz, Nicole Kidman, Julianne Moore, Kate Hudson, Sandra Bullock, Tom Hanks, Bonnie Hunt, Gary Sinise, Robert Redford, Al Pacino, Robert Downey, Jr., Gene Hackman, Michael J. Fox, Robert Redford, Julia Louis-Dreyfus, Paul Newman, Tom Cruise, Sally Field, Gene Hackman, Kim Basinger, Barbra Streisand, Chevy Chase, Robert De Niro, Glenn Close, Madonna, Meryl Streep, Oliver Stone, Whoopi Goldberg, Michael Douglas, Sylvester Stallone, Demi Moore, and many many others.

Ever on the cutting edge, CAA has a large new media department with eight agents dedicated to the Internet and technology clients.

Agents
George Lane and Michael Cardonick
Clients
Many many stars

⚞ Ginger Dicce Talent Agency ⚟

56 W 45th Street, #1100
just W of 5th Avenue
New York, NY 10036
212-869-9650

...of the few agents in town who still works exclusively freelance, Dicce says she still gives newcomers a chance and looks at every piece of mail that enters her office.

Starting as a secretary at Wells Rich Green, Ginger moved into production via her smarts and helpful mentors. Once she was producing and casting, she says she fell in love with actors and decided to become an agent.

She started her agency in 1986 and has been busily repping union and non-union actors ever since.

When I asked Ginger what attracted her to an actor she said it was a "gut inner thing" so your guess is as good as mine. Since Ginger suffers no fools, I wouldn't call her unless you are focused, business oriented and have some idea how you can be marketed.

Agent
Ginger Dicce
Clients
Freelance

⇢ DGRW ⇠
Douglas, Gorman, Rothacker & Wilhelm, Inc.

1501 Broadway, #703
btwn 43rd & 44th Streets
New York, NY 10036
212-382-2000

Flo Rothacker (Ann Wright), Jim Wilhelm (Lionel Larner, Eric Ross, The Barry Douglas Agency), Barry Douglas (ICM) and Fred Gorman (Bret Adams) created this effective, congenial agency in 1988.

Though Flo and Jim are the sole partners since Barry and Fred died in 1996, they have retained the four-partner name as a tribute to them. DGRW is as strong as ever, continuing as one of the best agencies in New York, across-the-board.

Although this agency has grown in stature and access, it has not sacrificed the nurturing elements that made it special to actors in the first place. Flo Rothacker still has the sensibilities that made her choose her first job at Ann Wright's agency due to its proximity to Bloomingdale's. She endures as one of New York's major musical comedy agents and is quoted at length throughout this book.

Jim Wilhelm has worn many showbiz hats since he began as a fifteen-year-old actor. He has been a stage manager, public relations director, general manager and a casting director before he finally became an agent in 1981.

Jim has a stellar reputation in New York working with diverse and well-respected actors especially in concerts, on network television and in major features. In addition to all his other activities, Jim finds time to teach master classes on the guest faculty at the University of Cincinnati/College Conservatory of Music and has taken on an adjunct position at NYU teaching the Business of Show Business for the young actor.

Michelle Gerard was a musical theater actress before she joined DGRW's agency training program. She is now an outstanding agent for musical theater (among other things) with what is reported to be an encyclopedic knowledge of musical theater history. She recently received her Masters in Arts Administration from NYU.

A former child performer, Josh Pultz moved to the Big Apple from upstate New York in 1998 to major in Psychology, but decided that he still really wanted to be in the business. A week later, he was interning at DGRW. Later, thinking he wanted to be a general manager, he left to work with producer Cameron Macintosh and general manager, Alan Wasser, but missed life at DGRW and returned in January of 2000 as an assistant.

..., ...p........ Zimbalist, and others.

DGRW also represents writers, directors, fight directors, choreographers and musical directors. Clients of this office who travel west to work are introduced to several agencies with whom the office has relationships. That way the actor and the agent have a chance to make the most compatible relationship.

DGRW sees new clients through referral only, although they do carefully study pictures and resumes. They are not interested in tapes produced for audition purposes only. While this is an agency of established actors, DGRW also prides itself on its development of new talent.

Agents
Jim Wilhelm, Flo Rothacker, Michelle Gerard, and Josh Pultz
Client List
100

Eastern Talent Alliance, Inc.

1501 Broadway, #404
btwn 43rd & 44th Streets
New York, NY 10036
212-840-6868

Eastern Talent Alliance, Inc. partners Allen Flannagan (The Allen Flannagan Agency, Michael Kingman Agency), and Carol Davis (Alliance Talent) officially ceased operation as the East Coast satellite of Alliance Talent in 1999 and have emerged as a force on their own.

Carol has pretty much become the one-stop shopping ground for Savion Glover and all the best tap dancers in town. Flannagan mostly handles administrative duties now and Eric Emery and Christine Kromer rep ETA's actors for theater, film and television.

Eric majored in theater at Ball State and got his first job within three days of arriving in New York. He turned it down four times until he got the money he wanted.

The actors' nomadic lifestyle didn't suit Eric's personality and since he was so great at business, he began researching agenting possibilities. He called Wendy Wetstein at Integrity Talent and became her first assistant, absorbing all her actor nurturing skills.

When Wendy closed shop for married life, Eric's next job was with Michael Hartig, one of the best negotiators in town and, in 1997, joined the team at Eastern Alliance Talent. Eric says his two mentor/role models both gave him the perfect grounding for his new life.

Christine Kromer was a casting intern while she was still in college, for Lynn Kressel Casting and on *As the World Turns*. When she was ready for a full-time job, she worked as an assistant at Writers & Artists and then cast an HBO movie before returning to the agenting side of the business at William Morris during 1998 and 1999.

Stints casting at Disney Touchstone Television and at Fox Casting preceded Christine's return to agenting at the beginning of the new millennium when she joined Eastern Alliance.

Clients from the list of eighty plus include Paige Price (*Saturday Night Fever*), Cathy Trien, Alix Korey (*Wild Party*), Jonathan Woodward (*Wit*), Doris Belack (*Tootsie*), Donna Mitchell (*Boiler Room*), and Shannon Walker Williams (*Girl Fight*).

Agents
Allen Flannagan, Carol Davis, Eric Emery, and Christine Kromer
Client List
80 plus

✎ EWCR ✐
Epstein-Wyckoff-Corsa-Ross & Associates

311 W 43rd Street, #1401
btwn 8th & 9th Avenues
New York, NY 10036
212-586-9110

Gary Epstein was still an actor when he began answering phones for his agent, Mort Schwartz. His part-time job began a journey that included a nine year association with the prestigious Hesseltine Baker Agency and gave him rigorous training for helming his own agency.

Gary Epstein started Phoenix Artists in 1986 and merged with Los Angeles agent Craig Wyckoff in 1991, giving both Gary and Craig visibility and offices for clients on both coasts. Today Gary represents not only actors, but writers and directors as well. Partner Randi Ross (Don Buchwald & Associates, J. Michael Bloom) shepherds young adults. Renee Panicelli heads up the Children and Young Adults division. George Mastrogiorgis helms the literary department.

EWCR sees clients mostly by referral, but checks pictures and resumes.

Agents
Gary Epstein, Randi Ross, and Renee Panicelli
Client List
less than 100

⚞ Jim Flynn, Inc. ⚟

aka Berman Boals & Flynn

208 W 30th Street, #401
btwn 7th & 8th Avenues
New York, NY 10001

~~~ ~~ ~~~ spring of 2003 and at that point, Judy and Jim reevaluated their eight year partnership and decided that each had grown to their point that they each wanted their own agency.

They were still friends and saw no reason to separate geographically, so now there are two separate offices in residence at 208 W 30th Street with two different styles, lists, goals, etc. This is good news to potential clients who now just have to manage to get one agent to fall in love with them instead of two.

Somehow Jim has managed to maintain a successful talent/lit agency and attend law school at the same time. In 2003, he earned the right to sign, 'Esq.' after his name. As a lawyer, he can add entertainment law to his list of services, a big plus for clients. Jim's list of actors includes Frank Wood and Enid Graham.

His clients come mostly through referrals. Although this office looks at all pictures and resumes, they rarely call anyone in from them.

Agents
Jim Flynn
Client List
30

FBI/Frontier Booking International, Inc.

1560 Broadway, #1110
at 46th Street
New York, NY 10036
212-221-0220

Established in 1979 by Ian Copeland, FBI emerged as one of the largest rock agencies around (Sting, Snoop Doggy Dog, Modern English, Jane's Addiction, etc.). At this point, the theatrical arm of the agency, started in 1984, has become the dominant presence.

John Shea (SEM&M and Kronick, Kelly & Lauren) heads up the theatrical department representing a hot list of young actors. Clients from that list include Alicia Minshew (*All My Children*), Darien Sills Evans (*On the One, Cosby*), Jacqueline Torres (*FX, Hack*), Sean Nelson (*Fresh, American Buffalo, The Corner*), Jessica Brooks Grant (*What Dreams May Come*), Sara Tanaka (*Rushmore, Old School*), Jonathan C. Kaplan (*Falsettos, The Graduate*), Sean Owens (*Cinematherapy*), and Steven Lee Merkel (*Escape from Experiment Island*).

Helping John run herd on this talented bunch are Heather Finn (Abrams Artists) and Rosa Fanelli (Young Talent Management).

FBI handles all types for all areas. They work with an extensive freelance list as well as with signed clients.

Agents
John Shea, Rosa Fanelli, and Heather Finn
Client List
60 plus freelance

☙ The Gage Group ❧

315 W 57th Street
W of 8th Avenue
New York, NY 10036
212-541-5250

scene for many years now, and although Martin headquarters on the West Coast, he spends enough time in New York to really know all the clients.

The dynamic duo that run the New York office, Phil Adelman and Steve Unger, are not only best friends, but their backgrounds and personalities are synergistic. A theater major, Steve taught high school after graduation and was pondering what interesting direction his background might take him. When he found The Gage Group, he knew he was home.

Phil was an elementary school teacher, quiz show writer, director, screenwriter, director of musicals, and a composer and lyricist. I can't think of anything Steve and Phil wouldn't be able to handle.

Wendie Relkin Adelman heads the commercial department. T h e client list at The Gage Group is filled with fabulous names like Paul Benedict, Walter Charles, Marilyn Cooper, Jane Connell, Dee Hoty, Gavin MacLeod, Debra Monk, John Cunningham, Marcia Lewis, Walter Bobbie, Liz Callaway, Nancy Ringham, Ernie Sabella, Edward Hibbert, Shirley Knight, Harriet Harris, Tovah Feldshuh, Phyllis Newman, Leslie Uggams, Beth Fowler, Chuck Wagner, and B.J. Crosby.

The Gage Group have been my agents for over twenty years. Although I live in California, I know all the New York office and love them dearly. When you see Phil's quotes elsewhere in this book, you will get an idea of how this office operates, but for starters, Phil told me he would never think of releasing a client just because he wasn't getting work. "When a client of mine doesn't get work, I just figure the people who are doing the hiring are morons." I know when I take on a client that it's for life. I have so much faith in my own taste that I would never lose faith in a client.

Agents
Phil Adelman, Steve Unger, and Martin Gage
Client List
65

⊿ Garber Talent Agency ⊾

2 Pennsylvania Plaza, #1910
7th Avenue btwn 32nd & 33rd Streets
New York, NY 10121
212-292-4910

about opening her own agency.

Well-connected in the casting community, Karen hit the ground running and is able to say that of her forty-six clients, at least 90% are currently employed.

Mark Fleischman (Joan Scott, Curtis Brown, EWCR) was a performer, casting director and manager before he became an agent. He came to GTA in 1999 bringing with him an impressive list of legit actors that balances nicely with Karen's musical comedy thrust giving added resonance to an agency that already had a strong client list.

Actors from their list include John Mineo (*Chicago*), Michael Kubala (*Chicago*), Jacqueline Knapp, Jane Lanier, Kurt Ziskie, Ed Hyland, Elena Ferrante (international company of *West Side Story*), and Birdie Hale (*Blind Faith.*)

Karen also sports a strong list of dancers and choreographers. This office works with signed clients theatrically, but does freelance for industrials and commercials. Although she does look at pictures and resumes, to get a call from this agency you will need a strong resume.

Agents
Karen Garber and Mark Fleischman
Client List
46

showcases only

≈ The Gersh Agency New York ≈

130 W 42nd Street, #2400
btwn 5th & 6th Avenues
New York, NY 10036
212-997-1818

The Gersh Agency New York was formed when Scott Yoselow, David Guc, Ellen Curren, and Mary Meagher decided to leave Don Buchwald & Associates to form a New York office for the legendary Phil Gersh.

Scott Yoselow, who heads up the literary department, is the sole remaining founding partner. Colleagues who represent GANY's illustrious list of actors are ex-casting executive, Lindsay Porter, William Butler (WMA), Stephen Hirsh (Paradigm), Jennifer Konawall, Sally Ware and Rhonda Price.

This agency prefers well-trained actors and is meticulous about monitoring new talent by attending showcases and readings. If you don't have a referral, concentrate on doing remarkable work in a showcase and ask them to come and see it.

The client list shared by The Gersh Agency on both coasts is outstanding. Their impressive client list includes Catherine Keener, Patricia Clarkson, Jeffrey Demunn, Mary Kay Place, Mena Suvari, Tobey Maguire, Kelli Martin, Gloria Reuben, Fran Drescher, David Schwimmer, Jane Krakowski, Roma Downey, Victor Garber, Dan Hedaya, Christopher Lloyd, Robert Prosky, Dan Futterman, and Kyle Secor.

The Gersh Agency New York continues the top level representation Phil Gersh pioneered for actors, writers, directors, authors, and below-the-line clients.

Agents
Lindsay Porter, William Butler, Stephen Hirsh, Jennifer Konawall, Sally Ware, and Rhonda Price
Client List
220 (NYC/LA)

⩗ HWA Talent Representatives ⩘

220 E 23rd Street, #400
btwn 2nd & 3rd Avenues
New York, NY 10010

⌐ne search took him to New Hampshire's Hampton Playhouse where J had been a teenage apprentice and now became their perennial summer general company and/or stage manager.

In the winters, he continued his search for his "place" in the business in NYC. He worked as business manager at the WPA, as an AD on a Broadway show and spent several years in ticket sales at the Metropolitan Opera, continually turning a deaf ear to the friends who kept telling him he'd make a great agent.

In 1990, he finally accepted his destiny and took a receptionist job at (now defunct) Select Artists which started him up the ladder. Just three years later, he was an agent at The Tantleff Office with Alan Willig before both moved to HWA in 1996.

Diana Doussant says she was "born in a trunk" in Germany where her father was an opera singer. Though she made her own stage debut at seven and later attended the High School of Performing Arts, Diana says she never had the self-motivational skills needed to be an actor, though her friends continued to tell her that she would make a great agent.

While working in group sales at Madison Square Garden in 1983, a friend's introduction to agent Tex Beha (STE, Paradigm) led Diana to iconic agent Jeff Hunter (Jeff Hunter, DHKPR, Triad, WMA) who became her mentor when she joined DHKPR.

A full agent just two years later, she agented at Abrams Artists until 1991 when she joined APA. When Diana left APA, she was "wooed" by Patty to join the HWA family.

The list of clients at the New York office is impressive. Among them are Joe Morton (*Bounce*), Christina Chang (*Dragnet*), JC MacKenzie (*Dark Angel*), Sian Phillips (*Old Lady, Marlena*), Karen Ziemba (*Contact*), Carolyn McCormick (*Law & Order*), John Benjamin Hickey (*It's All Relative, The Crucible*), Michael Berresse, Bill Nunn, Ian Kahn, Rosemary Murphy, Wallace Shawn, and Jeff Goldblum (NY only).

Many New York independent agencies have a liaison arrangement with a West Coast agency, but HWA manages to combine its own West Coast office (helmed by owner Patty Woo) with the offices and clients of another West Coast office, Gold Liedtke, expanding the possibilities for HWA clients and increasing the power and breadth of both agencies. HWA presides over a combined Los Angeles/New York list of about 250 theatrical clients as well as those of GL.

The commercial department is led by Mary Collins and Brian Holtzberg. New clients come to this agency mainly by referral.

Agents
Diana Doussant, J Kane and Patty Woo
Client List
250 combined coasts

⊿ Peggy Hadley Enterprises, Ltd. ⊿

250 W 57th Street, #2317
btwn 7th & 8th Avenues
New York, NY 10107

more actors to her list and became an agent.

She has about sixty to seventy signed clients and works with many others freelance. She handles only legit, no commercials.

In 2000, when Peggy hired actor Chris Nichols to be her assistant, Chris says the two of them "just clicked." Nichols is now her colleague and their synergy has expanded the agency to establish a new Young Performers Department adding some young faces to the agency.

Clients from their list include Lou Meyers, Dick Latessa, Clifford David, Jason Patrick Sands (*The Producers*), Kara Cooper (*Urban Cowboy, Harmony*), and Danette Holden (*Laughing Room Only, The Sound of Music*).

Agents
Peggy Hadley and Chris Nichols
Client List
60-70

⚜ Harden-Curtis Associates ⚜

850 7th Avenue, #903
btwn 55th & 56th Streets
New York, NY 10019
212-977-8502

After working together for fifteen years at Bret Adams, Mary Harden and Nancy Curtis decided it was time to put their own philosophies into practice at their own agency. That was in 1996 and the partnership continues to work like gangbusters with Nancy heading the theatrical division and Mary helming the important literary division.

Nancy studied acting for seven years as a child, but since her parents felt she should pursue a real job with her Master's Degree from Michigan State University in advertising, she worked at Leo Burnett in Chicago and at Ted Bates in New York.

A wise colleague finally suggested that since Nancy was more addicted to reading plays than *Advertising Age*, perhaps her interests lay elsewhere.

Once in the agenting business, her acting/marketing background propelled her quickly from Bret Adams' assistant to his colleague.

Mary's early career was spent problem solving with writers and actors in a variety of jobs at various regional theaters, giving her the perfect background to work with both at HCA.

Nancy and Mary each have mantras of sorts. Mary feels communication is the key to a successful actor-agent relationship along with a strong career plan. Nancy's envisions her advice to all clients written on her tombstone: Run your own company!

I agree wholeheartedly with both.

In addition to Mary and Nancy, HCA clients have two other champions: Diane Riley, whose background includes worked in casting at The Roundabout Theater Company and assisting company management at the Goodspeed Opera House and ex-actor Michael Kirsten whose theater degree is from Northwestern. Both have been at HCA since 1997.

The fab four represent about 150 signed clients including Kathryn Hays (*As the World Turns*), Andrea Anders, (*Spellbound, The Graduate*),

Rider Strong (*The Graduate, Cabin Fever*), Peter Hermann, Veanne Cox (*Caroline or Change*), Damon Gupton (*Deadline*), Dennis Kelly (*Urinetown*), Sharon Wilkins (*Bad Boys 2, Maid in Manhattan, Two Weeks Notice*), David Alan Basche (*Three Sisters*), Bruce Norris (*Sixth Sense, School of Rock*), Corey Reynolds (*Hairspray*, Tony Award nominee), Kate Shindle (*Stepford Wives, Cabaret*), and Ginnifer Goodwin (*Mona Lisa Smile, Win A Date with Tad Hamilton*).

Harden Curtis

⊿ Henderson-Hogan Agency Inc. ⊾

850 7th Avenue, #1003
btwn 56th & 57th Streets
New York, NY 10019
212-765-5190

Maggie Henderson formed her first agency with Joan Scott in 1967. When Scott moved on to create Writers & Artists in 1967, Maggie established The Henderson Agency and Jerry Hogan joined her.

An actor who decided against the instability of the actor's life, Hogan worked as a private secretary to actress Margaret Leighton before his first job in the agency business at Dudley, Field & Malone Agency. He was a commercial agent at New York's United Talent before joining Maggie. A year later, Jerry became her partner and Henderson-Hogan was born.

When HH became bicoastal in 1974, Maggie moved west while Jerry headed the New York office. Maggie died in 1996 and Henderson-Hogan/Los Angeles ceased to exist in 1999.

Though no longer bicoastal, Hogan's clients are not homeless in Los Angeles as Hogan works intimately with several agencies there, including Ann Gettys and Conan Carroll.

George Lutsch (who trained at HH) joins Jerry in representing clients like Dakin Matthews (*The Fighting Temptations*), Trace Thomas (*Wonderfalls*), Christopher Fitzgerald (*Wickett*), Peggy Pope (*Law & Order, Ed*), Earl Hyman (*Euripides*), and Cynthia Mace (*Ice Bound*).

Although HH prefers to work with signed clients, they do occasionally freelance with former clients and/or old friends.

Agents
Jerry Hogan and George Lutsch
Client List
60 plus

⊯ Independent Artists Agency ⊯
aka Carlson-Menasche Artists

159 W 25th Street, #1011
btwn 25th & Seventh Avenues
New York, NY 10001

Thus, in 1992, Jack became an assistant at one of Manhattan's busiest theatrical agencies at the time, Ambrosio/Mortimer. The small, but visible client list gave the agency credibility and Jack a perfect platform from which to learn the business. Two years later, Jack joined APA as assistant to agent David Kolodner and learned even more.

Jack went back to A/M briefly before taking a break from that side of the business to return to acting. It didn't take long for Jack to re-evaluate his priorities and choose agenting as the path he truly wanted. In July of 1997, he opened his own office.

His impressive client list is a result not only of scouting new talent at comedy clubs, showcases and workshops, but the largess of talent available when Ambrosio/Mortimer went out of business. Since Jack already had relationships with many of those actors, they were eager to do business with his new agency.

From the beginning, Jack had the trust of the casting directors in town and they sent some fine clients his way also. His first pilot season, he booked three actors and was off and running.

From 1999 until 2003, Jack partnered with Philip Carlson (Susan Smith Agency, Writers & Artists), but when Philip decided to leave the business and return to his hometown of Seattle, Jack changed the name of the agency and decided to go it alone.

Associate Jessica Noujaim was an actress before joining Jack to help rep his list of about fifty clients. Their list includes Marisa Ryan (*Riding in Cars with Boys*), Barney Hughes, Helen Stenborg, Idris Elba (*The Wire*)

Robert Lupone, Timothy Adams (*One Life to Live*), Daniel Von Bargen, Melissa Leo (*Homicide, 21 Grams*), and Lois Smith.

Jack says his agency is open to developing new young talent and seriously looks at all pictures and resumes and is not deterred by an actor not having his union card: They have to start someplace.

Agents
Jack Menasche and Jessica Noujaim
Client List
50

⚞ Ingber & Associates ⚟

274 Madison Avenue
btwn 39th & 40th Streets
New York, NY 10016
212-889-0450

Amy Davidson was a child actor in Los Angeles before attending
NYU Tisch School of the Arts majoring in acting and directing. She
knew all along that she wanted to agent though and joined Carole right
out of NYU.

Although I&A is a commercial agency, I include them because they
specialize in handling commercial careers of working actors. If you are
already working good jobs as an actor and are looking for someone to
handle the commercial part of your business, Carole may be the woman
to talk to.

This agency also handles a few industrials and some print jobs for
their clients.

Agents
Carole Ingber and Amy Davidson
Client List
160 plus freelance

ᴀ Innovative Artists ᴄ

235 Park Avenue South
btwn 19th & 20th Streets
New York, NY 10003
212-253-6900

Gersh alums Howard Goldberg and Scott Harris opened the New York edition of their prestigious Los Angeles agency, Harris and Goldberg, in 1991. A prestigious boutique agency from the get-go, the agency has now grown into one of the most important independent agencies on either coast. Scott now helms the Los Angeles office while Richie Jackson heads up operations in New York.

Richie, former assistant to showbiz dynamo Harvey Fierstein, joined IA in 1993 as an assistant and quickly blossomed into the head of the dynamic New York office handling theater, film, television, literary, voiceovers, beauty, commercials, and broadcasting.

Clients include Edie Falco (*The Sopranos*), John Amos (*John Q*), Bryce Dallas Howard (*The Woods*), Kate Nelligan (*Cider House Rules*), Frances Fisher (*Unforgiven*), Patti LuPone (*Summer of Sam*), Jason Biggs (*American Wedding*), Alicia Silverstone (*Scooby-Doo 2*), Traci Lords (*First Wave*), Alyson Hannigan (*American Wedding*), Katherine Bell (*JAG*), Illeana Douglas (*Missing Brendan*), Kelly Hu (*X-Men 2*), Lorraine Bracco (*The Sopranos*), Jill Clayburgh (*Leap of Faith*), Doris Roberts (*Everybody Loves Raymond*), Peter Boyle (*Everybody Loves Raymond*), Elliot Gould (*Ocean's Eleven*), Gary Busey (*Quigley*), Jeremy Sisto (*Six Feet Under*), and Andrew McCarthy (*Kingdom Hospital*).

Clients are seen at this agency strictly by referral.

Agents
Richie Jackson, Gary Gersh, Allison Levy, Lisa Lieberman, Suzette Bazquez, Eddie Mercado, Jana Kogen, Sue King, Michael Shea, Jennifer Jackino, Barbara Coleman, Donna Gerbino, Maury DiMauro, and Ross Haime
Client List
Large

✍ Innovative at Ford Models ✍

142 Green Street, 4th floor
off 10th Avenue & Spring Streets
New York, NY 10012
212-219-6190

They are currently not accepting any pictures/resumes by mail or by drop off but it doesn't hurt to check for the moment when their current crop "age" out of their system.

Agents
Melissa Cardona, Arlene Weiss, and Alison Luscombe
Clients
A large and lovely list

⟋ ICM/International Creative Management ⟍

40 W 57th Street
just W of 5th Avenue
New York, NY 10019
212-556-5600

Just like actors, talent agencies have good years and bad years. ICM's stars (both astrological and theatrical) are currently in flux.

✦ *Julia Roberts, the first actress to earn $20 million a picture, has severed ties with her talent agency, International Creative Management, where she'd been a client since 1991.*

No reason was publicly offered for the move, nor was it clear whether Roberts would sign on elsewhere. Since her longtime agent, Elaine Goldsmith-Thomas, left to become a partner in Revolution Studios in October 2000, the Oscar-winning actress (Erin Brockovich) had been represented by ICM Chairman Jeff Berg.

The move is a major blow to ICM, particularly since Cameron Diaz followed her agent, Nick Styne, to Creative Artists Agency last year.

The agency still represents a chunk of Hollywood talent, however, including Denzel Washington, Mel Gibson, Michelle Pfeiffer and Richard Gere.

Elaine Dutka, *Los Angeles Times*[20]

The powerful Jeff Berg leads the agency through showbiz's changing tides and ICM will surely survive with such clients as Chris Rock, Cher, Judy Davis, Marg Helgenberger, Helen Mirren, Maggie Smith, Brad Garrett, John Mahoney, Kim Cattrall, Cheryl Hines, Stockard Channing, Lena Olin, Gena Rowlands, Kathy Bates, Paul Newman, Sam Waterston, Dennis Miller, Jay Leno, Peter MacNicol, Vanessa Redgrave, Ellen DeGeneres, Henry Winkler, Marlee Matlin, Woody Allen, Garry Marshall, Mel Gibson, Eddie Murphy, Jodie Foster, James Woods, Henry Winkler, John Larroquette, Christian Slater, and Downtown Julie Brown.

Variety queried studio execs for a feature in October 2001 as to who were the top agencies:

◆ *In a tight race, CAA came out slightly ahead, followed by Endeavor, UTA, William Morris and then ICM. Overall, on a four-point scale, only one-half point separated No. 1 and No. 5.*
    Claude Brodesser, *Variety*[21]

If you are hot and deciding which of the star agencies to choose, go to the *Variety* archives online at www.variety.com or to the Motion Picture Academy Library and look up the article.

Agencies large and small tend to be

Agents
Sam Cohn, Boaty Boatwright, Paul Martino, Andrea Eastman, Bart Walker, Mitch Douglas, and many many others
Client List
3,400

◢ Jordon Gill & Dornbaum Agency, Inc. ◣

1133 Broadway #623
at 26th Street
New York, NY 10010
212-463-8455

Robin Dornbaum and Jeffrey Gill, owners of this hot thirty-year-old agency specializing in children, were both under twenty-five when they bought the agency in 1988.

Although Robin loved actors and wanted to work with them in some way, she never knew how until, as a communications major, she spent six months interning with the legendary Marje Fields. Robin knew quickly she had found her calling. After six months, mentor Fields sent her to work in casting at Reed Sweeney Reed, where she worked for free, honing her skills, storing information and growing in the business.

When she graduated from school and began casting six months later, Sweeney introduced her to the Joe Jordon Agency which at that time only represented adults. Jordon's son, Vance (now a famous art gallery owner), soon focused the agency onto the lucrative children's marketplace.

Vance hired a prominent children's agent and Robin became her assistant. When the agent left two years later, Vance had to decide between selling the agency or revitalizing it in some way. He opted for a new management team promoting Robin to agent and luring child agent specialist Jeffrey Gill (Bonni Kidd, Fifi Oscard) to be her partner.

Robin and Jeff's youth, savvy and industriousness changed this agency into one of the top kid agencies in New York.

Jan Jarrett (Jan J Agency) merged her agency with JG&D in October in 1999 and now heads up the legit department. David McDermott (FBI, HWA) was an actor before becoming an agent so you can be sure he knows just what you are going through. He reps the eighteen to thirty age group.

Jeff and Robin head the commercial department. JGD has sixty to seventy signed clients and works extensively with managers.

Prospective clients should send in snapshots, not professional pictures. Clients include Emily Mae Young (*Step by Step*), Michael

Angarano (*For Richer or Poorer*), Patrick Levis (*So Weird*), Angelo Massagli (*The Sopranos, Stuart Little 2*), Greg Siff (*From Justin to Kelly*), Jimmy Pinchack (*Family Affair*), Kristino Sisco (*As the World Turns*), and Adam Zolotin & Justin Restivo (*Leave It to Beaver*).

Agents
Jan Jarrett and David McDermott
Client List

⚞ Stanley Kaplan Talent ⚟

139 Fulton Street, #503
btwn Broadway and Nassau
New York, NY 10038
212-385-4400

Stanley Kaplan gets people jobs. Originally a regular employment agent, Stanley's introduction to agents via his son's involvement in acting, let him to switch gears and start getting jobs for actors.

For a while Kaplan represented non-union talent as an agent before becoming a manager. In 1998, Kaplan got his franchise from SAG and now has access to union actors and union jobs.

When I asked Stanley how big his client list was, he spread his arms and said, "I represent the entire city of New York! I'm the agent for the underdog. Anyone who can't get an agent can come here. I submit everybody. It means something to be able to go into an agent's office. I'm here for actors."

Stanley reps people across the board, any age, any type, any ethnicity, any job, extras, commercials, print, television. Any medium that might be using actors, Stanley's there.

Agent
Stanley Kaplan
Client List
The City of New York!

⚓ Kerin-Goldberg Associates ⚓

155 E 55th Street, #5D
btwn 3rd & Lexington Avenues
New York, NY 10022
212-838-7373

chum Gary Epstein cajoled her into joining his office and becoming an agent. Goldberg's path has also included stints with Henderson-Hogan, Bonni Allen and ultimately, Coleman-Rosenberg. Although Charles was working at another agency when he was called on to broker a literary deal for one of C-R's theatrical clients, he and Ellie hit it off immediately and spoke often of opening their own agency when the time was right.

1995 turned out to be the magic year when Kerin and Goldberg got together to create this classy agency representing actors, playwrights, directors, composers, choreographers, songwriters, scenic designers, costume designers and art directors.

Ellie, Charles and colleagues Ron Ross (Waters Nicolosi) and Donald Birge (newly franchised at KGA) represent a prestigious list of big name, working actors like Jean Stapleton, Austin Pendleton, and Donald Sadler who grace their client list. They see new clients only by referral but do look at all pictures and resumes.

There are incisive comments from Ellie elsewhere in the book. Be sure to check them out.

Agents
Charles Kerin, Ellie Goldberg, Ron Ross and Donald Birge
Client List
100

⚔ Archer King, Ltd. ⚔

317 W 46th Street, #3A
btwn 7th & 8th Avenues/across from Joe Allen's
New York, NY 10036
212-765-3103

Archer King has been a showbiz fixture forever. The Internet Broadway Database (www.IBDB.com) lists him as producing *Two Blind Mice* on Broadway with Melvyn Douglas in 1949, so this gentleman of the theater has been here for a while. At one time or another, I think Archer has either worked with or discovered everyone in the business.

He left producing to agent with the legendary Louis Shurr Agency, repping the big musical stars of the day, as well as Bob Hope. Archer opened his own agency in 1957 and still has files on Jason Robards, James Dean, James Coburn, Martin Sheen and the three-year-old Ronny Howard, all actors he helped at the beginning of their careers.

From 1963-67, Archer got involved with foreign films importing and distributing such films as Roman Polanski's *Knife in the Water* and Volker Schöndorff's *The Tin Drum*, as well as films from Ingmar Bergman.

While head of theater for RKO Television, he was responsible for the television productions of *The Gin Game* starring Hume Cronyn and Jessica Tandy, and *Sweeney Todd* starring Angela Lansbury (for which Archer won a Golden Ace Award).

Although some guides list Archer repping actors, comedians, composers, directors, legitimate theater, lyricists, packaging, producers, screenwriters and musical theater, Archer says his main business these days is developing and packaging movies.

He works with a select group of actors, still has a perceptive eye for talent, and is known to give newcomers a helping hand.

Agent
Archer King
Clients
Freelance

⚞ The Krasny Office, Inc. ⚟

1501 Broadway, #1303
btwn 43rd & 44th Streets
New York, NY 10019
212-730-8160

own in late 1991. He found office space not only in the same building, but on the same floor where he had worked with Craig Anderson years before.

Gary's background, experience and taste made him a favorite with the casting community, so when he opened his office, he quickly became part of the mainstream.

B. Lynne Jebens (Michael Hartig) and Gary run the legit department along with newly franchised agent, Christine Iobst.

Iobst's background in theater and dance is a plus for the agency. She joined the office as an intern while still in college, moved up to became their assistant and is now their colleague.

The Krasny Office continues to thrive and grow. Clients from their list include Denny Dillon (*Dream On*), Jennifer Laura Thompson (*Urinetown*), Carl Gordon, Meg Mundy, and Ken Jennings.

The Krasny Office has liaison arrangements with several Los Angeles agents and managers.

Norma Eisenbaum (Sharon Ambrose) runs the highly successful commercial, voiceover and print department.

Agents
Gary Krasny, B. Lynne Jebens, and Christine Iobst
Client List
85

✎ LTA/Lally Talent Agency ✎

Film Center Building
630 9th Avenue, #800
at 44th Street
New York, NY 10038
212-974-8718

Dale Lally was an actor and personal manager before he crossed the desk to became an agent. He worked for Mary Ellen White and Nobel Talent before partnering with print agents Wallace Rogers and Peter Lerman (Lally Rogers & Lerman).

When Lally, Rogers and Lerman decided to go their separate ways in 1992, Dale opened this office.

Partner Stephen Laviska was a contract lawyer before he joined Dale, representing their strong list of musical performers, interesting young adults and solid character people.

Actors from their list include James Lally, Angel Caban, Alice Spivak, Timothy Warmen, Jerome Preston Bates, Eric Michael Gillett, Raymond Jaramillo Mcleod, Brenda Denmark, and Victor Anthony.

Agents
Dale Lally and Stephen Laviska
Client List
45

⚐ The Lantz Office ⚑

200 W 57th Street, #503
at 7th Avenue
New York, NY 10019
212-586-0200

Clark Gable, Madeleine Carroll and other illustrious stars until William Morris bought that company a year later.

Lantz worked for smaller agencies for a few years before opening Robert Lantz, Ltd. in 1954. A year later, he succumbed to Joe Mankiewicz's pleas to join his efforts producing films. It took three years for Lantz to figure out that he found agenting a much more interesting profession.

In 1958, Lantz reentered the field as a literary agent. Feeling that a mix of actors and directors and writers gave each segment more power, his list soon reflected that.

Dennis Aspland worked for the legendary Sam Cohn before joining The Lantz Office to represent screenwriters, directors and actors.

I really only include this agency to save you postage since The Lantz Office only handles two actors, longtime clients Liv Ullman and Polly Holiday.

The main thrust of the agency continues to be writers and directors.

Agents
Robert Lantz and Dennis Aspland
Client List
20

⚔ Lionel Larner, Ltd. ⚔

119 W 57th Street, #1412
btwn 6th & 7th Avenues
New York, NY 10019
212-246-3105

Lionel Larner is one of the classiest agents in town both in demeanor and client list. His first job in the business was as European casting director for Otto Preminger on the film, *St. Joan*. When he turned in his casting hat for that of an agent, he was trained by CAA's legendary Martin Baum while they were both at GAC. In 1969, when Lionel left Baum and GAC (now ICM), he started Lionel Larner, Ltd.

Not only did Lionel start at the top, he has remained there with prestigious clients like Madeleine Potter, Dorothy Loudon, Diana Rigg, Simon MacCorkindale, and Stacy Keach and, though now a member of Parliament, Glenda Jackson is still technically an actress.

LL is not strictly a star agency. Lionel represents actors on every level and admits to being a real snob about his clients, demanding that they have impeccable theater backgrounds.

Well, why not? He does. One of the perks of this book has been meeting people like Lionel who return phone calls, are responsible, creative, caring, and have taste, style, stature, and access.

Agents
Lionel Larner
Client List
40

⊿ Leading Artists, Inc. ⊾

aka Silver Massetti & Szatmary East Ltd./West Ltd.

145 W 45th Street, #1204
btwn 6th & 7th Avenues
New York, NY 10036

Happy key-catcher Dianne Busch came to New York from Ohio in 1979 figuring to act but within three months was stage managing, producing and ultimately supervising messengers at the TKTS booth on 47th Street.

She moved to California to work at Western Stage in Salinas before the Big Apple lured her back two years later for a cross-section of showbiz jobs ranging from commercial casting with Joy Weber and colleagues Judy Rosensteel and Jackie Fink

Another casting stint, this time with Meg Simon and Fran Kumin, preceded a career as a manager and ultimately led the way to Monty in 1991. Eleven years later, in 2002, in a Christmastime announcement, Dianne was named Monty's choice to head the agency upon his retirement.

Mark Upchurch (Peter Strain, Henderson Hogan, J. Michael Bloom) joined the agency in 1999. Stacy Baer arrived in 2001 after agent-assisting at Paradigm and casting at Warner Bros. on *Third Watch*.

Clients from their list of about 85 include Chuck Cooper, Michael Lombard, Jordan Charney, Gerrit Graham, E. Katherine Kerr, Paul Guilfoyle, James Rebhorn, Zeljko Ivanek, Celeste Holm, Fyvush Finkel, Michael Gross, Burke Moses, Daniel Jenkins, Larry Pine, Robert Joy, Jackie Hoffman, Adriane Lenox, Amy Acker, Jeremiah Miller, Jenna Stern, Wayne Kasserman, Darren Ritchie, Aasif Mandvi, Bradley White, and Tricia Paoluccio.

Leading Artists remains closely affiliated with Monty's former Los

Angeles partners, Donna Massetti and Marilyn Szatmary (now SMS Talent), with whom they continue a "sisterly" bicoastal relationship much as they did when the agency was one.

Agents
Dianne Busch, Stacy Baer, and Mark Upchurch
Client List
85

☄ Leudeke Agency ☄

1674 Broadway, #7A
btwn 52nd & 53rd Streets
New York, NY 10019
212-765-9564

about starting an adult department at her agency. Penny shared space with Pat for a year before opening her own office.

Victor Varnado (*The Adventures of Pluto Nash*), ex-pro football player David Roya (the bad guy in the *Billy Jack* movies), Ashley Howard Wilkinson (*Smokey Joe's Cafe, Creature*), and Deidre Goodwin (*Chicago*) are a few names from her list.

In addition to representing actors, the Leudeke Agency has a thriving literary department helmed by Elaine Devin. Elaine was a story editor and worked in development before she formed her own literary management company which has now become a part of Leudeke, repping writers and directors.

Penny lists premiere American baritone Sherrill Milnes, legendary jazz sax players James Moody and Kenny Barrett, classical composer Anthony Davis (*Angels in America)* and various writers, dancers and singers as part of her professional family.

Penny looks carefully at all pictures and resumes and has found a couple of her most successful clients that way.

Agent
Penny Leudeke
Client List
50

⚞ Bruce Levy Agency ⚟

311 W 43rd Street, #602
btwn 8th & 9th Avenues
New York, NY 10036
212-262-6845

"Life is an adventure" should be emblazoned on the forehead of Bruce Levy. An actor, producer (*The Price of Genius*) and entrepreneur, Levy opened his own agency in 1992 and, on opening day, found himself up to his ears in work and in actors.

A man who doesn't know how to do things halfway, Bruce gives the kind of attention that has attracted actors with important resumes. Motivated actors inspire him to even greater heights.

Bruce is interested in making money for himself and his clients, but his quest is for quality. Actors with the same mind set will find a happy and rewarding relationship with the Bruce Levy Agency. Bruce is especially drawn to offbeat and unusual actors. Bruce says he specializes in ethnic and character looks.

Although he works chiefly with signed clients, Bruce works briefly with freelance talent as a prelude to signing. Two from his list are Sylvia Miles and Mark Baker.

Agents
Bruce Levy
Client List
30

◢ Bernard Liebhaber Agency ◣

352 Seventh Avenue
btwn 29th & 30th Streets
New York, NY 10001
212-631-7561

Bernard Liebhaber has been in show business in one form or

David Drummond. In 1996, Bernard decided it was finally time to open his own agency.

Timothy Nolen (*Phantom of the Opera*), Gordon Elliott (*Follow that Food*), Stanley Wayne Mathis (*Kiss Me Kate*), and opera star Julia Migenes are clients on his list of about thirty-five to forty.

Liebhaber works with no freelance talent and usually finds clients via referral although he does check out pictures and resumes that come to him.

Agents
Bernard Liebhaber.
Client List
35-40

⚞ Nicolosi & Co. Inc. ⚟

150 W 25th Street, #1200
btwn 6th & 7th Avenues
New York, NY 10001
212-633-1010

Jeanne Nicolosi is an awesome woman. After getting her B.A. in acting from the University of Massachusetts and M.A.s in acting and directing from Emerson College, she headed the theater department and taught acting at a Boston high school.

Though she moved to New York to act and direct and was successful at both, neither lifestyle appealed to her. She wondered what it would be like to be an agent and her first exposure, as an assistant agent with Beverly Anderson, convinced her she was on the right path.

In 1985, Jeanne became a franchised agent, working briefly at Writers & Artists before joining The Bob Waters Agency where she quickly became a partner. Wanting her own agency from the start, Nicolosi finally realized her dream in 2002.

Nicolosi met all the first year goals she set for herself. It was obviously time for her dreams to come true. Colleague Russell Gregory leads both the Young Performer/Developing Clients and the Daytime Department while John Woodward (Nanni Saperstein Management), who has a built-in radar for emerging filmmakers, gives the agency a presence in the thriving NYC independent film scene.

Clients from their amazing list include Michael Goduti (*State Side*), John Highsmith (*School of Rock*), Johnny Pruitt (*Sponk, Whirly Girl*), Jeff Weiss (*Flesh & Blood*), Jenny Fellner (*Mamma Mia, The Boy Friend*), John Michael Bolger (*Third Watch*), Miles Purintan (*Dogville*), and two new stars to be, Lauren Hotcher, and Michael Cohen.

Agents
Jeanne Nicolosi, John Woodward, and Russell Gregory
Client List
60-65

⤳ Nouvelle Talent, Inc. ⤶

20 Bethune Street, #5A
in the Village, W of 8th Avenue
New York, NY 10014
212-352-2712

.... p.......uons, so if you
nave any musical ability and/or a one person show, or have put
together any other kind of entertainment, Toni might be able to find
some bookings for you.

Until 1997, the New York office was run by associate, B. G. Gross,
but at that time, Toni decided to move to New York and run this office
herself.

Toni has decided to return to her maiden name, Toni (Antoinette)
Sipka, but was known for years as Ann Bordalo and says she answers
to either.

Pictures that catch her eye feature a nice smile, are clean, crisp,
warm, neat and professional. Toni looks for a sexy wholesomeness in
women clients instead of the fresh-scrubbed look and seeks men with
a well-groomed look and likes a length shot. Toni is one agent who likes
to be called weekly and quizzed as to "What's going on?" When talent
calls Toni, she says she knows they are interested in working. If they
don't call, she tends to forget about them.

Nouvelle sounds like an exceptional resource.

Agents
Toni Sipka
Client List
Large

⚞ Omnipop ⚟

55 West Old Country Road
Hicksville, NY 11801
516-937-6011

Though I couldn't have imagined Long Island as a spawning ground for an influential showbiz agency, Omnipop has managed to spawn and then some. Tom Ingegno (pronounced "engine-yo"), Ralph Asquino and Bruce Smith started this agency on Long Island in 1983 and, from the beginning, they prospered.

An eclectic lot, the Omni partners are all stand-up performers, musicians or managers who booked themselves and their friends on college circuits and later, clubs. As they graduated to bigger, more diverse venues and clients, starting an agency was a logical progression. Omnipop consciously chooses staff that share this background.

Their taste and savvy led them to create their own niche representing stand-up comics for personal appearances, television, film and commercials.

In their one concession to tradition, Bruce moved to Los Angeles to open a West Coast headquarters in 1990. Tom runs things on Long Island. He says that having an office away from Manhattan allows them to spend less time commuting and more time doing their work. Tom says they still come into the city: "We go out and scout a lot of people and develop them. We discover a lot of talent in New York because a lot of comedy comes from here."

Omni's clients were once exclusively stand-up performers but today their list contains very well trained comedic and legit actors, usually with a background in improv or sketch comedy, and many are refugees from The Groundlings.

The bottom line at Omni is still, "talented and interesting people who have something to offer."

Although the Los Angeles office is only interested if you have already spent at least a year in the business and are playing a decent venue, the East Coast office see themselves as the farm team, developing the stars of tomorrow, so they're a little more approachable. You still really should have twenty to thirty minutes worth of material before you query this agency as a stand-up.

Clients routinely work *The Tonight Show, The Late Show with David Letterman, E! Entertainment, Late Night with Conan O'Brien*, clubs, film, theater and some, like Christopher Titus (*Titus*), Teresa Strasser (*While You Were Out*), Derek Waters (*Married to the Kellys*), and Christopher Moynihan (*Coupling*) either have their own series or are series regulars.

Omnipop has their own cool web page filled with information about all their clients and the agency, so if you want to know more about these guys, check out www.omnipop.com .

There are some helpful insights from Bruce and Tom ~~~~

~~~~ ~~~~ ~~~~background interesting, they will either ask to see a tape or come see you work.

Agents
Tom Ingegno, Ralph Asquino, Simon Hopkins, and Barbara Klein
Client List
40-50 combined NY/LA list

⊿ Fifi Oscard Agency, Inc. ⊵

110 W 40th Street, #1601
btwn 6th & 7th Avenues
New York, NY 10018
212-764-1100

Fifi Oscard was a frustrated housewife and mother in 1949 when she began working gratis for Lee, Harris, Draper. When I asked her in what capacity she was working, she said, mostly as a jerk but added that in nine months she was no longer inept and had worked herself up to $15 a week. Always interested in theater and with the ability to do almost anything, Fifi has prospered.

Today she holds forth over a giant agency that represents actors, authors, directors, producers, composers, playwrights and singers in all areas of entertainment and publishing. Fifi continues to be the same warm, shrewd Earth Mother I encountered early in my career and still comes into the office every day.

Peter Sawyer and Francis Del Duca represent their list of respected actors that includes William Shatner, Ken Howard, Jean Marsh, Leon Redbone, Tony Musante and Marcia Wallace.

The children's department is headed by Pace University grad, French-born Julien Rouleau, who began his agenting career as an intern at FOA. Kevin McShane heads the commercial department.

The agency handles about 200 signed clients for theater, film, and television, and services freelance people mainly in the courtship stage before signing them. Actors may send photos and resumes but please don't send reels unless they are requested.

Agents
Fifi Oscard, Carmen La Via, Peter Sawyer, Francis Del Duca, and Julien Rouleau
Client List
200

◿ Dorothy Palmer Talent Agency, Inc. ◺

235 W 56th Street, #24K
btwn 7th & 8th Avenues
New York, NY, 10019
212-765-4280

Dorothy Palmer T...

...ncert and Artists Corporation before starting her own agency in 1974.

Dorothy's list includes entertainers, actors, writers, producers, broadcasters, comedians, dancers, singers, models, television hosts, and hostesses and senior citizens, many of whom are hyphenates like actress-impersonator Holly Farris, actor-broadcaster Mike Morris, actor-writer Anthony King, actor-producer Robert Capelli, J. J. Reep, Frank Gorshin (*Goodnight Gracie*), Captain Lou Albano (*The Cannibals*), Michael Sawsett, Michael Caruso, Matthew Lavin, and Michele Muchler.

Dorothy enlarged the agency recently, adding a literary franchise which will possibly benefit her actor clients as well as her screenwriters.

Since Dorothy is seriously committed to the plight of independent filmmakers, she is also always looking for investors and has packaged a new film starring client Frank Gorshin and Tony Curtis called *Pizza with Bullets*.

Agents
Dorothy Palmer
Client List
A dozen plus freelance

⚞ Meg Pantera, The Agency ⚟

1501 Broadway #1508
btwn 43rd & 44th Streets
New York, NY 10036
212-278-8366

Meg Pantera was running her own theater in 1990 when she fell in love with one of her directors and followed him to New York. In addition to love, one does need money, so when a friend suggested that she would make a good agent, she met with Bob Barry (Barry Haft Brown).

Tentative about agenting, she signed on part-time but quickly warmed to her new life as an agent. She was franchised at Bob's in 1995 and speaks glowingly of him as an agent, mentor and role model. Meg opened her own office in January 2000.

Although Meg has about seventy-five clients with whom she has exclusive agreements, you won't find a long list of names if you check out the SAG agent/client directory. She feels the partnership between an actor and an agent is forged by mutual work on the career not by pieces of paper.

Clients with this arrangement include Glenn Cruz (*Plan B*), Drew Sarich (*The Hunchback of Notre Dame*), Brant Carroll (*Footloose, Potluck*), Nathan Lee Graham (*Sweet Home Alabama, Zoolander*), Gene Silvers (*Law & Order*), and Ramsey Faragallah (*Strip Search*).

Meg's list is ethnically mixed and she submits clients without regard to ethnic breakdowns. New clients come to Meg mostly via referral from other clients and from casting directors. Whether an actor has his union card or not doesn't make any difference to Meg if she thinks you are talented. Meg works with a few freelance clients.

She also represents the legendary film director, Sydney Lumet.

Agent
Meg Pantera
Client List
75

⤳ Paradigm ⤶

500 5th Avenue, 37th floor
at 42nd Street
New York, NY 10110
212-703-7540

more power, class and stature to an already topline agency. New York Paradigm theatrical agents include Sarah Fargo (Writers & Artists), Richard Schmenner (STE) and Rosanne Quezada. Schmenner and Quezeda were both franchised at this agency.

Paradigm serves British clients in England as well as those in New York and Los Angeles. Their actors appear to be happy and loyal; Brian Bedford has been Clifford's client for over thirty years.

Other names from their prestigious list include Philip Seymour Hoffman, William Baldwin, Charles Durning, Andy Garcia, Campbell Scott, Laurence Fishburne, Eli Wallach, Anne Jackson, Dana Ivey, Max von Sydow, Allison Janney, Chris Cooper, and Dennis Franz.

Agents
Clifford Stevens, Richard Schmenner, Sarah Fargo, and Rosanne Quezada
Client List
60

⚐ Professional Artists ⚑

321 W 44th Street, #605
btwn 8th & 9th Avenues
New York, NY 10036
212-247-8770

Sheldon Lubliner is fun, easy to talk to, informed, a good negotiator and he has a good client list. Add charm, taste, ability, access and a great partner, Marilynn Scott Murphy, and you've pretty much got a picture of Professional Artists.

As a director-producer, Sheldon enjoyed all the details involved in mounting shows for Al Pacino, Gene Barry and Vivica Lindfors; he just didn't like raising the money.

Deciding he could transfer all his skills into agenting and not be a fundraiser, Sheldon changed careers in 1980 translating his contacts and style into an agency called News and Entertainment. PA is an outgrowth of that venture.

Actress/client Marilynn Scott Murphy was commandeered to answer phones in a pinch in 1986 and has since become Sheldon's partner. Sheldon's negotiating skills and Marilynn's people skills, although they are both strong in this department, form the perfect agent.

Their colleague, Ohio native Kevin Hale, got his degree from Wright State University in directing and worked as an assistant to the producer of North Shore Music Theater in Beverly, Massachusetts before he made it to the Big Apple.

When he got to town, a friend told him Sheldon and Marilynn were looking for someone to answer phones and the rest is history. He moved from phone answerer to assistant and is now their colleague.

Their list includes not only actors, news and radio personalities but also writers, producers, directors, and casting directors.

Agents
Sheldon Lubliner, Marilynn Scott Murphy, and Kevin Hale
Client List
100

⤜ Gilla Roos, Ltd. ⤛

16 W 22nd Street, 3rd floor
just W of 5th Avenue
New York, NY 10010
212-727-7820

Her son, David, who now runs the business, was a chef when his mother first conscripted him to work with her. He kept going back to cooking, but his mom ultimately prevailed and now, David says, his wife is a better cook than he is.

GR was already a commercial force when they lured Marvin Josephson (APA, Gage Group) away from Hartig-Josephson in 1984 to create what has become a very well-regarded legit department.

Marvin entered the business as an office boy for the great literary agent Audrey Wood and, in addition to reading scripts and running the switchboard, was able to observe the careers of such literary stars as Tennessee Williams, William Inge, Carson McCullers, and Robert Anderson.

Clients on Marvin's list include Samuel E. Wright (*The Lion King*), Mamie Duncan Gibbs (*Chicago*), Harry Goz (*Fiddler on the Roof*), Diana Pappas (*The Full Monty*), Vince Trani (*Kiss Me Kate, Phantom of the Opera*), Michael Hayward-Jones (*Les Miz*), Sara Pramstaller (*Saturday Night Fever*), Carol Lynley, Polly Adams, David Carradine, and Chuck Stransky.

Agent
Marvin Josephson
Clients
35

➶ Schiowitz/Clay/Rose, Inc. ➴

165 W 45th Street, #1210
btwn 6th Avenue and Broadway
New York, NY 10036
212.840.6787

Originally a producer and general manager, Josh Schiowitz (Los Angeles productions of *Nuts, Sister Mary Ignatius, Pump Boys & Dinettes, Uncommon Women & Others* and *Cloud 9*), took his formidable marketing and organizational skills, his connections to casting directors and talent, and ultimately transformed from buyer to seller when he opened SCR in 1987.

Stephen Rose and Josh Clay were his partners for a while and although the masthead retains their names, Schiowitz is the sole owner.

Teresa Wolf (Honey Sanders, Penny Leudeke, Waters Nicolosi) was an actor before Honey hired her to be an agent. She joined SCR's New York office nine months after it opened in February 2000. Wolf says she has lived all over the country but has been in NYC longer than anywhere else although she says this still doesn't make her a native.

Colleague Kevin Thompson has a background not only in agenting (Honey Sanders) but in casting and then stage managing for fourteen years at both Long Wharf and the Hartford Stage. He joined SCR in January 2003.

Clients from their New York list include Mary Bond Davis (*Hairspray*), Marva Hicks (*Caroline or Change*), George McDaniel (*Big River*), Marin Ireland (*Harlequin Studies*), Rebecca Wisocky (*36 Views*), James Biberi (*Analyze That*), Colman Domingo (*Henry V*), and Anne O'Sullivan (*Mere Mortals*).

SCR says if they specialize in anything, it is in really good actors. Though they review all pictures and resumes, they admit they rarely call anyone in from a mailing. The client list is a combination of referrals and heavy theater credits.

Agents
Teresa Wolf and Kevin Thompson
Client List
70

➣ Ann Steele Agency ➣

330 W 42nd Street, 18th floor
btwn 8th & 9th, W of Port Authority
New York, NY 10036
212-629-9112

Houst....

...g young actors like Jason Alexander, Michael E. Knight, Kevin Kilner, Alex Winter, and Christopher Steele.

Ann retired from managing in 1989, reemerging as an agent in 1997 with ASA. She has about 120 signed clients for theater, film, television and commercials who range in age from twenty-one to seventy plus.

Her eclectic list includes Joe Abraham (*Hairspray*), Deliso Beeks (*Aida*), Barney Cheng (*Wasabi Tuna, Hollywood Ending*), James Darrah (*Some Like It Hot*), Colleen Hawks (*The Boy from Oz*), Gayle Holsman (Denver's Ovation Award for Best Actress in a Musical), Peter Kapetan (*Aida*), Melissa Mahon (*The Producers*), Orville Mendoza (*Aladdin Live* at California Adventure), Jody Reynard (*Taboo*), Elizabeth Share (*Mamma Mia*), Kenny Williams (*The Lion King*) and Gene Jones who is a featured voice in the two new Ken Burns documentaries: *Jack Johnson* and *Horatio's Drive*.

While I was there, a client called and said she was in the neighborhood and would Ann like a nice iced coffee? How can you not love a client like that? And how can you not love an agent who is known in some circles as Ragtime Ann?

Agent
Ann Steele
Client List
120

⚞ Stone Manners ⚟

900 Broadway, #803
btwn 19th & 20th Streets
New York, NY 10003
212-505-1400

The offspring of a famous British agent, Tim Stone came to Los Angeles in 1979 establishing his own agency, UK Management, providing services for British actors in this country. Although he used his British list as a base in the beginning, Tim's list quickly expanded to represent a much broader base.

By 1982, Tim acquired partner Larry Masser (Stone Masser) and by April 1986, Scott Manners (Fred Amsel, Richard Dickens Agency) name was added to the masthead (Stone Manners Masser). By August, Larry left and since 1986, the partnership of Tim and Scott has prevailed.

In January 2003, at a time when many NYC agencies were closing, Stone Manners was doing so well that they decided to open an East Coast office. Tim moved to Manhattan and Scott keeps the business in tact in Los Angeles.

Stone Manners represents a prestigious list of actors, directors, producers, scriptwriters, young adults and teens. SM won't let me name anyone from their list so you'll have to check SAG's agency files or scan the *Players Guide* to check out their clients.

Agents
Tim Stone
Client List
They won't say

Peter Strain & Associates, Inc.

1501 Broadway, #2900
btwn 43rd and 44th Streets
New York, NY 10036
212-391-0380

Coast haven for clients working both coasts, the New York office continues as strong as ever and is in the capable hands of Bill Timms and Bill Veloric.

Though Bill Timms' community theater background back in Scranton helped him land a freelance arrangement with Writers & Artists shortly after arriving in town in 1984, it didn't prepare him for the pain of rejection.

Hugely disappointed when, after four callbacks, he was still not chosen for a coveted job, Bill quietly presented himself to his agents at Writers & Artists and told them that he felt he would be more successful on the other side of the desk.

From W&A, Bill went to The New York Agency, Sames & Rollnick, and onto The Tantleff Office before joining Strain.

Since Bill Veloric's dad was an agent back home in Philadelphia, he knew early on that he wanted to rep performers. A band singer as a kid, he headed to the Big Apple straight from high school and at nineteen worked at the fabled Hesseltine-Baker Agency repping an A- list of Manhattan's theater talent. He worked for manager Yvette Schumer and agent Fifi Oscard before becoming a twenty-six-year old franchised agent at Epstein Wykoff.

He moved to Los Angeles where he worked for CNA (now Diverse Talent Group), The Artists Group and Stone Manners. He finally succumbed to homesickness and began searching for a way to return to New York. In June 2003, Peter Strain offered him the chance not only to return but to renew a fifteen year friendship with Timms.

This agency is home to Joe Mantegna, Frank Langella, Emily Loesser, Lewis J. Stadlen, Rene Auberjonois, Jonathan Hadary, Corey Parker, Brent Barrett, Adam Storke, Bryan Batt, Norm Lewis, Robert Sella, Lewis Cleale, Ron Bohmer, Gerry Bamman, Mary Louise Wilson, Marlo Thomas, Georgia Engel, Rebecca Schull, Marylouise Burke, Eileen Brennan, Carolee Carmello, Emily Skinner, Valerie Perrine, Randy Graff, Alma Cuervo, Catherine Cox, and Heather Macae.

Although most clients come to this office by referral, the Bills say they look at pictures and resumes religiously.

Agents
Bill Timms and Bill Veloric
Client List
70

✄ Talent House ✄

311 W 43rd Street, #602
(at 8th Avenue)
New York, NY 10036
212-957-5220

Dave works in conjunction with his Toronto counterparts, owner-founder Bruce Dean and former Vice- President of Creative and Casting for Livent, Beth Russell.

The agency handles actors, directors, choreographers, and writers for theater and musical theater and at some point, for film and television.

They avoid freelancing and prefer referrals from actors seeking representation. Names from their list include Jeremy Kushnier and Shannon Lewis.

Agents
Dave Bennett
Client List
60

⤏ Talent Representatives, Inc. ⤎

20 E 53rd Street, #2A
just E of 5th Avenue
New York, NY 10022
212-752-1835

Honey Raider and Steve Kaplan's mutual love of theater, film, and television led them to create this agency as a way to become involved in show business. The agency formed in 1964 to represent actors has now grown to include writers, directors and producers.

Honey says the changes came about through a natural change of events as some actors who worked daytime shows decided to write and ended up being staff writers and those writers became producers, etc.

Now, Talent Representatives is one of the few agencies that does a real literary business in daytime.

Honey's list of clients is confidential so you'll need to do some research at SAG or with the *Players Guide* to see who they are.

Agents
Honey Raider and Andrew Stocker
Client List
17 plus freelance

⨀ WMA/William Morris Agency ⨀

1325 Avenue of the Americas
at 54th Street
New York, NY 10019
212-586-5100

new William Morris.

♦ *[Wiatt] oversees an agency that has 235 agents and claims about 4,000 clients worldwide in offices in Beverly Hills, New York, London and Nashville.*
Claudia Eller and James Bates, *Los Angeles Times*[22]

Wiatt brought with him such clients as Eddie Murphy, Sylvester Stallone, William Friedkin, Nora Ephron, Renny Harlin, Richard Donner, Neil Simon, Tim Allen, Lauren Shuler Donner, Lorne Michaels and two of ICM's most prized agents, David Wirtschafter and senior literary agent Amy Ferris.

Along with wanting to continue his professional relationship with Wiatt, Wirtschafter (who joins as an Executive VP and a member of the board) was drawn to the new William Morris management structure. The new William Morris seeks to establish a business where all parties report to each other, bypassing a more elite hierarchy.

Establishing the new William Morris has not been pain-free. The decision to consolidate the talent portion of the motion picture department in Los Angeles hit the New York office hard as many dyed in the wool New Yorkers had no intention of relocating to Los Angeles.

What remains after the many changes, is a sleeker, more powerful, less bureaucratic agency that reps not only actors, writers, directors and producers, but athletes, newscasters, political figures and almost any other being of notoriety. If having the most agents means you have the most power, William Morris wins hands down. On a list of agents I looked at, William Morris had 222 as compared to 94 at ICM and 113 at CAA.

In any event, the number of agents is staggering. I'm not going to attempt to list all the names as the list is way too long and supposedly confidential. The *Hollywood Creative Directory* somehow manage to penetrate the iron curtain, so for a detailed up to the minute list of names, check it out. The *HCD* tracks the names of conglomerate agents effectively.

William Morris may or may not be #1 as of this writing, but perennially, at Oscar time, when the big agencies take out ads to congratulate their nominees, William Morris has the longest most impressive client list.

Robert Duvall, Billy Bob Thornton, Willem Dafoe, Forest Whitaker, Daniel Day-Lewis, Christopher Walken, Emma Thompson, Matthew Modine, Lili Taylor, Ashley Judd, Cary Brokaw, Robert Altman, John Rubinstein, John Travolta, Bruce Willis, Julianne Moore, Tim Burton, Clint Eastwood, Stephen Frears, Diane Keaton, John Malkovich, Alec Baldwin, Danny Aiello, Charlie Sheen, Dean Stockwell, Bill Cosby, Sean Hayes, Ray Romano, Alfre Woodard, and Candice Bergen are just some of William Morris's amazing list.

Jeff Hunter heads the film department.

Agents
Jeff Hunter, David Kalodner, Bill Contardi, Claudia Cross, Owen Laster, Marcy Posner, Kenny Goodman, Bill Liff, Steve Speigel, Mark Subias, and others
Client List
4,000 worldwide

❧ Hanns Wolters International ❧

10 W 37th Street, 3rd floor
just W of 5th Ave.
New York, NY 10018
212-714-0100

unofficial son, helping him not only recover from Marianne's death but also refocus his business. Oliver, who now owns HWI, ultimately supported Hanns through his own lengthy fatal illness.

The agency is currently experiencing a rebirth of sorts seeing more actors on Broadway with some of their literary talent represented at Sundance and other film fests.

HWI is still one of the places casting directors call for European actors and is also known for its strong New York character types. Every week you'll see HWI clients on episodic television shot in New York. Their commercial success is impressive, too, with clients booking Coke and Gateway.

Although HWI works with about 300 clients, they say there is a core group of thirty that gets most of the calls. These actors are not only talented but also network and help keep the calls coming in.

This agency doesn't sign contracts with its clients preferring to work on a handshake basis. One of the "handshakes" belongs to Karen Lynn Gorney from *Saturday Night Fever*.

They also represent German cinema on the East Coast. Amongst HWI's illustrious projects was last year's Academy Award winning Best Foreign Language Film, *Nowhere in Africa*.

Agents
Oliver Mahrdt
Clients
Freelance/union plus non-union

◢ Ann Wright Representatives ◣

165 W 46th Street, #1105
just E of Broadway, in the Equity Building
New York, NY 10036
212-764-6770

When Ann Wright came to New York after training as an actress at prestigious Boston University, she joined the casting pool at CBS. Like many other actors who have an opportunity to explore other areas of the business, she realized there were other ways to use her creative skills and became the assistant to legendary William Morris agent, Milton Goldman.

Ann cast commercials at an advertising agency and then worked for both Charles Tranum and Bret Adams before opening her own commercial talent agency in 1964.

Still thought of first as a voiceover and commercial talent agency, the legit department continues to thrive with clients working in theater, film and television.

Her theatrical list includes Etain O'Malley, Billie Allen, Herab Rubens, and David de Vries (*Beauty and the Beast*).

Agents
Ann Wright
Clients
20

Glossary

Academy Players Directory — Catalogue of actors published annually

the union covering actors for work in the theater state you must have a verifiable Equity Contract in order to join, or have been a member in good standing for at least one year in AFTRA or SAG.

Initiation fee is $1000 as of 4/03, payable prior to election to membership. Basic dues are $118 annually as of 11/03. Additionally, there are working dues: 2% of gross weekly earnings from employment is deducted from your check just like your income tax.

Actors' Equity Minimum— There are eighteen basic contracts ranging from the low end of the Small Production Contract to the higher Production Contract covering Broadway houses, Jones Beach, tours, etc. Highest is the Business Theater Agreement, for industrial shows produced by large corporations. All monies are discussed online at "contracts" at www.actorsequity.org.

Actor Unions — There are three: Actors' Equity Association (commonly referred to as Equity) is the union that covers actors' employment in the theater. The American Federation of Television and Radio Artists (commonly referred to as AFTRA) covers television and radio actors, broadcasters and recording artists. Screen Actors Guild (commonly referred to as SAG) covers actors employed in theatrical motion pictures and filmed television. The unions continue discussions about the potential of joining together under one overall labor organization.

AFTRA Membership Requirements — anyone expecting to work in the news and entertainment industries can join. AFTRA's initiation fee is $1300 as of 11/03. Minimum dues for the first six-month period are $60. After joining, a member's dues are based on earnings in AFTRA's jurisdictions during the prior year. Dues are billed each May and November. For information on contracts, log onto www.aftra.org.

AFTRA Minimum — Check AFTRA's web page for rates.

AFTRA Nighttime Rates — Check AFTRA's web page for rates.

Atmosphere — another term for background performers, a.k.a. Extras.

Audition Tape — Also known as a Composite Cassette Tape. A videotape usually no longer than six minutes, showcasing either one performance or a montage of scenes of an actor's work. Agents and casting directors prefer tapes of professional appearances (film or television), but some will look at a tape produced for audition purposes only. Usually on VHS.

Background Performers — a.k.a. Atmosphere or Extras.

Breakdown Service — Started in 1971 by Gary Marsh, the Service condenses scripts and lists parts available in films, television and theater. Expensive and available to agents and managers only.

Clear — The unions require that the agent check with a freelance actor (clearing) before submitting him on a particular project.

Composite Cassette Tape — See Audition Tape.

Equity-Waiver Productions — See Showcases.

Freelance — Term used to describe the relationship between an actor and agent or agents who submit the actor for work without an exclusive contract. New York agents frequently will work on this basis, Los Angeles agents rarely consent to this arrangement.

Going Out — Auditions or meetings with directors and/or casting directors. These are usually set up by your agent but have also been set up by very persistent and courageous actors.

Going to Network — Final process in landing a pilot/series. After the audition process has narrowed the list of choices, actors who have already signed option deals have another callback for network executives, usually at the network. Sometimes this process can include ᵐˡ ᵃ ᶠ ᵗᵇ ᵇᵉᵉᵈ ᵒᶠ ʷᵇᵃᵗᵉᵛᵉʳ studio is involved.

The Leagues — A now defunct formal collective of prestigious theater schools offering conservatory training for the actor. There is no longer a formal association, but the current "favored" schools are still referred to by this designation. As far as agents are concerned, this is the very best background an actor can have, other than having your father own a studio.

Schools in this collective are The American Conservatory Theater in San Francisco, CA; American Repertory Theater, Harvard University in Cambridge, MA; Boston University in Boston, MA; Carnegie Mellon in Pittsburgh, PA; Catholic University in Washington, DC; The Juilliard School in New York City, NY; New York University in New York City, NY; North Carolina School of the Arts in Winston-Salem, NC; Southern Methodist University in Dallas, TX; The University of California at San Diego in La Jolla, CA; and the Yale School of Drama in New Haven, CT. Addresses are listed in Chapter Four.

Letter of Termination — A legal document dissolving the contract between actor and agent. Send a copy of the letter to your agent via registered mail, return receipt requested, plus a copy to the SAG and all other unions involved. Retain a copy for your files.

Major Role/Top of Show — See Top of Show.

Open Call — refers to audition or meeting held by casting directors that are not restricted by agents. No individual appointments are given. Usually the call is made in an advertisement in one of the trade newspapers, by flyers, or in a news story in the popular press. As you can imagine, the number of people that show up is enormous. You will have to wait a long time. Although management's eyes tend to glaze over and see nothing after a certain number of hours, actors do sometimes get jobs this way.

Overexposed — Term used by nervous buyers (producers, casting directors, networks, etc.) indicating an actor has become too recognizable for their tastes. Frequently he just got off another show after which everyone remembers him as that character and the buyer doesn't want the public thinking of that instead of his project. A thin line exists between not being recognizable and being overexposed.

Packaging — This practice involves a talent agency approaching a buyer with a writer, a star, usually a star director and possibly a producer already attached to it. May include any number of other writers, actors, producers, etc.

Paid Auditions — There's no formal name for the practice of rounding up twenty actors and charging them for the privilege of meeting a casting director, agent, producer, etc. There are agents, casting directors and actors who feel the practice is unethical. It does give some actors who would otherwise not be seen an opportunity to meet casting directors. I feel meeting a casting director under these circumstances is questionable and that there are more productive ways to spend your money.

Per Diem — Negotiated amount of money for expenses on location or on the road per day.

Pictures — The actor's calling card. An 8x10 glossy or matte print black and white photograph.

Pilot — The first episode of a proposed television series. Produced so that the network can determine whether there will be additional episodes. There are many pilots made every year. Few get picked up. Fewer stay on the air for more than a single season.

Players Guide — Catalogue of actors published annually for the New York market. Shows one or two pictures per actor and lists credits and representation. If you work freelance, you can list your name and service. Some list union affiliation. Casting directors, producers and whomever else routinely keeps track of actors use the book as a reference guide. Every actor who is ready to book should be in this directory.

agent.

Resume — The actor's ID; lists credits, physical description, agent's name, phone contact and special skills.

Right — When someone describes an actor as being right for a part, he is speaking about the essence of an actor. We all associate a particular essence with Brad Pitt and a different essence with Jim Carrey. One would not expect Pitt and Carrey to be up for the same part. Being right also involves credits. The more important the part, the more credits are necessary to support being seen.

Rollcall — similar to *Players Guide* and *Academy Players Directory* except pictures and information are fed into subscribers' computers. One advantage is you can update your resume as often as you like. There are many differing opinions on this. Some agents think it's stupid. I don't see the harm. It doesn't cost that much to be listed and many important buyers subscribe.

Scale — See salary minimums of each union.

Screen Actors Guild Membership Requirements — The most prized union card is that of the Screen Actors Guild. Actors may join upon proof of employment or prospective employment within two weeks or less of start date of a SAG signatory film, television program or commercial.

Proof of employment may be in the form of a signed contract, a payroll check or check stub, or a letter from the employer on company letterhead. The document must state the applicant's name, Social Security number, name of the production or commercial, the salary paid in dollar amount, and the dates worked.

Another way of joining SAG is by being a paid up member of an affiliated performers' union for a period of at least one year, having worked at least once as a principal performer in that union's jurisdiction.

The SAG initiation fee as of 7/03 is $1,406. This seems like a lot of money (and is) but the formula involved makes some sense. It's the SAG daily minimum of $678 times two, plus $50 for the biannual dues. For recorded information on how to join SAG call 323-549-6772.

This money is payable in full by cashier's check or money order at the time of application. The fees may be lower in some branch areas. SAG dues are based on SAG earnings and are billed twice a year. Those members earning more than $5,000 annually under SAG contracts will pay 1.5% of all money earned in excess of $5,000 up to a maximum of $150,000. If you are not working, you can go on Honorary Withdrawal which only relieves you of the obligation to pay your dues. You are still in the union and prohibited from accepting non-union work.

Screen Actors Guild Minimum — As of 7/03, SAG scale is $678 daily and $2,352 weekly for employment in films and television. Overtime in SAG is considerably higher than in AFTRA.

Showcases — Productions in which members of Actors' Equity are allowed by the union to work without compensation are called Showcases in New York and 99-Seat Theater Plan in Los Angeles. Equity members are allowed to perform, as long as the productions conform to certain Equity guidelines: rehearsal conditions, limiting the number of performances and seats, and providing a set number of complimentary tickets for industry people. The producers must provide tickets for franchised agents, casting directors and producers.

Sides — The pages of script containing your audition material. Usually not enough information to use as a source to do a good audition. If they won't give you a complete script, go early (or the day before), sit in the office and read it. SAG rules require producers to allow actors access to the script if it's written.

Stage Time — Term used to designate the amount of time a performer has had in front of an audience. Most agents and casting executives believe that an actor can only achieve a certain level of confidence by amassing stage time. They're right.

Submissions — Sending an actor's name to a casting director in hopes of getting the actor an audition or meeting for a part.

terms of your contract to stay for the ~~~~~ ~~~~ one-year options.

Top of Show/Major Role — A predetermined fee set by producers which is a non-negotiable maximum for guest appearances on television episodes. Also called Major Role Designation.

The Trades — *Back Stage* and *Ross Reports* are newspapers that cover all kinds of show business news. Los Angeles counterpart is *Back Stage West*. All list information about classes, auditions, casting, etc. These publications are particularly helpful to newcomers. In Los Angeles, this term refers to *Variety* and *Hollywood Reporter*. All are available at good newsstands, by subscription, or at the library.

Under Five — An AFTRA job in which the actor has five or fewer lines. Paid at a specific rate less than a principal and more than an extra. Sometimes referred to as Five and Under.

Visible/Visibility — Currently on view in film, theater or television. In this business, it's out of sight, out of mind, so visibility is very important.

99-Seat Theater Plan — The Los Angeles version of the Showcase. Originally called Waiver. Producers give actors an expense reimbursement per performance. It's not much, but at least you're not working for free.

Producers must also conform to Equity guidelines regarding rehearsal conditions, number of performances, complimentary tickets for industry, etc. If you participate in this plan, be sure to stop by Equity and get a copy of your rights.

⚒ 17 ⚒
⚒ Indexes/Endnotes ⚒

◢ Agents & Agencies ◣

⚑ Agents for Children & Young Adults ⚐

⚑ Agents for Stand-Up ⚐

⊿ Photographers/Resources/Teachers ⊾

⨀ Web Addresses ⨀

⚼ Everything Else ⚼

☒ Endnotes ☒

1. "The Early Bird Gets the Audition," March 23, 1995

2. "The Early Bird Gets the Audition," March 23, 1995

3. "The Careerist's Guide to Survival," April 25, 1982

9. "Out from the Shadows," January 13, 2000

10. "Hiding in Plain Sight," May 1997

11. "Out of the Woods," November, 1994

12. "Out of the Woods," November, 1994

13. "Agents Get Tough Grades from Pic Producers," October 3, 2001

14. "J. Lo: Ex-manager violated," July 3, 2003

15. "Vardalos' Ex-manager Dealt Lawsuit Setback," September 17, 2003

16. Silman-James Press, 2002

17. "Do Re ME Me Me!," November 10, 1997

18. "CAA: Packaging of an Agency," April 23, 1979

19. "Tenacious tenpercenters," April 7, 2003

20. "Julia Roberts leaves ICM," April 30, 2003

21. "Agents Get Tough Grade from Film Producers," October 3, 2001

22. "The Biz: William Morris Snags Jim Wiatt, Former ICM Exec," August 10, 1999

About The Author

Actress-author K Callan began writing her series of show business reference books in 1986 because, after many years in the business, she still did not know the answer to the question: *If every agent in the world wanted you, how would you make an intelligent decision?*

Now, all these years and thirty-something books later, Callan still calls agents, researches the business for actors, writers, and directors, and delights in learning more about the process of the business on stage and off.

Callan is a member of the Academy of Motion Picture Arts and Sciences, the Academy of Television Arts and Sciences, and a past member of the Screen Actors Guild Board of Directors.

Her acting career began in school plays in Texas and has continued through off-Broadway, films, and television. Her most visible television role to date was playing Superman's mom on ABC's hit series *Lois & Clark: The New Adventures of Superman.*

Callan's mothering career, in addition to her own three grown children, includes the likes of Michelle Pfeiffer in *Frankie & Johnnie,* Tom Hanks in *Bosom Buddies,* and Geena Davis in *Sara.*

Her big break came in 1971 with her first film, *Joe.* Her portrayal of Peter Boyle's subservient wife brought her glowing reviews in the *New York Times.* Other films include *A Touch of Class* with Glenda Jackson and George Segal, *American Gigolo* with Richard Gere, and *The Onion Field* with James Woods.

A regular on three network television series and a guest star in scores of television movies, miniseries and episodes, Callan also makes time to get back to the theater and is a member of the Classical Contemporary American Playwrights housed at Inside at The Ford in Los Angeles.

In addition to this latest expanded and updated edition of *The New York Agent Book,* Callan has written such other successful how-to tomes as *How to Sell Yourself as an Actor, The Los Angeles Agent Book, Directing Your Directing Career, The Life of the Party,* and *The Script is Finished, Now What Do I Do?*